A-Z LOUGHB

Key to Map Pages	2-3	Index
		Villag
Map Pages	4-41	and s

REFERENC[E]

Motorway	**M1**	Airport	✈
A Road	A36	Car Park (selected)	🅿
B Road	B3111	Church or Chapel	†
Dual Carriageway		Cycleway (selected)	🚴
One-way Street		Fire Station	■
Traffic flow on A Roads is also indicated by a heavy line on the driver's left.		Hospital	🅗
		House Numbers (A & B Roads Only)	13 8
Road Under Construction		Information Centre	🅸
Opening dates are correct at the time of publication.		National Grid Reference	⁴50
Proposed Road		Park & Ride	Birstall **P+R**
Restricted Access		Police Station	▲
Pedestrianized Road		Post Office	★
Track / Footpath		Safety Camera with Speed Limit	�30
Residential Walkway		Fixed cameras and long term road works cameras. Symbols do not indicate direction.	
Railway	Station / Level Crossing / Tunnel / Heritage Station	Toilet	
		without facilities for the Disabled	▽
		with facilities for the Disabled	▼
Built-up Area	MILK ST	Viewpoint	米 ✳
Local Authority Boundary		Educational Establishment	▢
Posttown Boundary		Hospital or Healthcare Building	▢
Postcode Boundary (within Posttown)		Industrial Building	▢
		Leisure or Recreational Facility	▢
		Place of Interest	▢
Map Continuation	▲ 15	Public Building	▢
		Shopping Centre & Market	▢
		Other Selected Buildings	▢

SCALE
1:15,840
4 Inches (10.16 cm) to 1 mile
6.31 cm to 1 km

0	¼	½	¾ Mile
0	250	500	750 Metres	1 Kilometre

Copyright © Geographers' A-Z Map Co. Ltd.

Telephone: 01732 781000 (Enquiries & Trade Sales)
01732 783422 (Retail Sales)

© Crown copyright and database rights 2015 Ordnance Survey 100017302.

Safety camera information supplied by www.PocketGPSWorld.com.
Speed Camera Location Database Copyright 2015 © PocketGPSWorld.com

Every possible care has been taken to ensure that, to the best of our knowledge, the information contained in this atlas is accurate at the date of publication. However, we cannot warrant that our work is entirely error free and whilst we would be grateful to learn of any inaccuracies, we do not accept responsibility for loss or damage resulting from reliance on information contained within this publication.

A-Z A-Z A**z** AtoZ
registered trade marks of Geographers' A-Z Map Company Ltd

www./az.co.uk

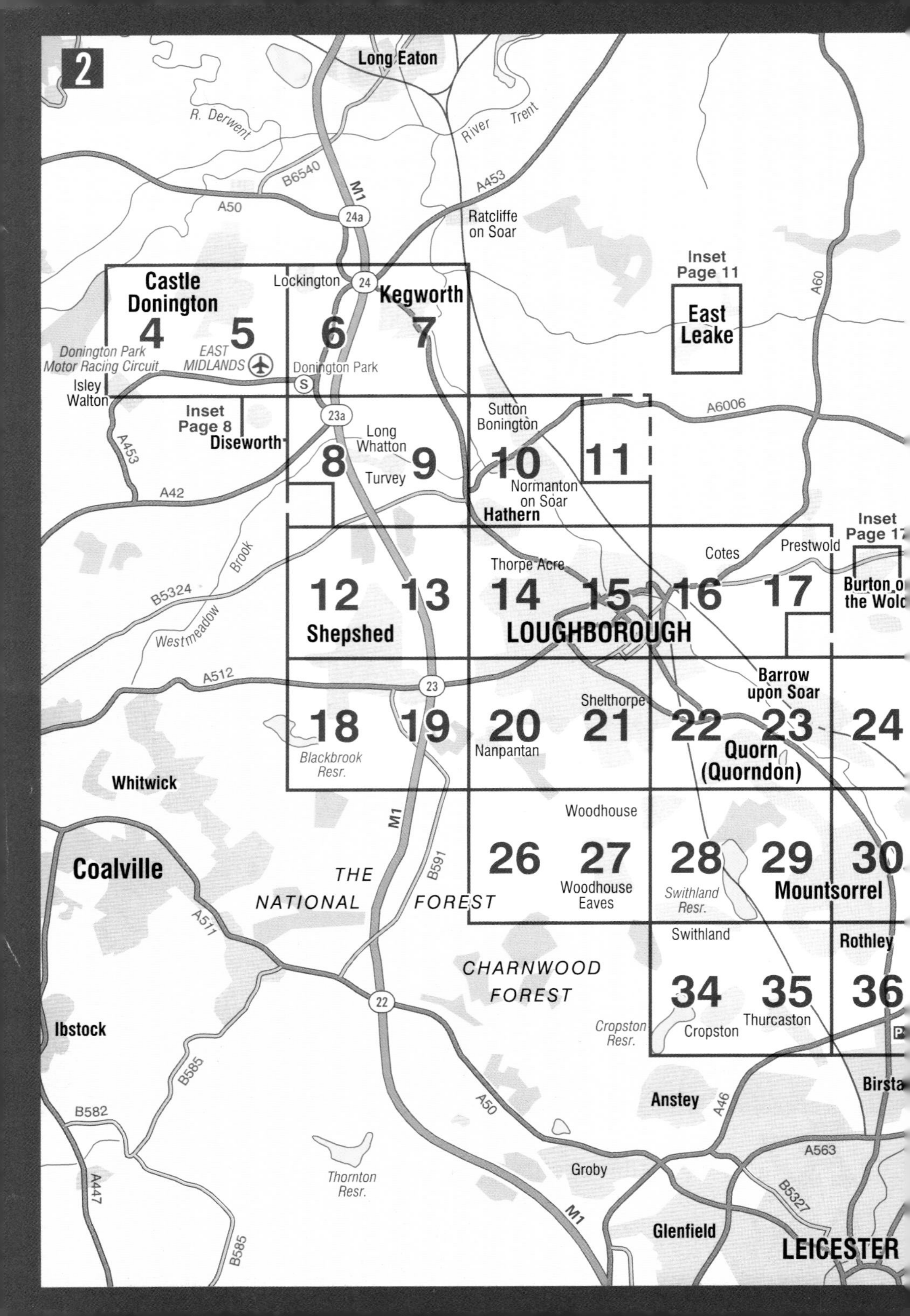
Long Eaton
R. Derwent
River Trent
B6540
M1
A453
A50
24a
Ratcliffe on Soar
Inset Page 11
East Leake
A60
Castle Donington
Lockington
24
Kegworth
4 5 6 7
Donington Park Motor Racing Circuit
EAST MIDLANDS
Donington Park
Isley Walton
Inset Page 8
Diseworth
23a
Long Whatton
Turvey
8 9 10 11
Sutton Bonington
Normanton on Soar
Hathern
A6006
A453
A42
Brook
B5324
Westmeadow
Thorpe Acre
Cotes
Prestwold
Inset Page 17
12 13 14 15 16 17
Shepshed
LOUGHBOROUGH
Burton on the Wold
A512
23
Shelthorpe
Barrow upon Soar
18 19 20 21 22 23 24
Blackbrook Resr.
Nanpantan
Quorn (Quorndon)
Whitwick
Woodhouse
M1
B591
26 27 28 29 30
Coalville
THE NATIONAL FOREST
Woodhouse Eaves
Swithland Resr.
Mountsorrel
A511
Swithland
Rothley
CHARNWOOD FOREST
22
34 35 36
Cropston Resr.
Cropston
Thurcaston
Ibstock
B585
Anstey
A46
Birsta
B582
A50
A563
A447
Groby
Thornton Resr.
B5327
M1
Glenfield
B585
LEICESTER

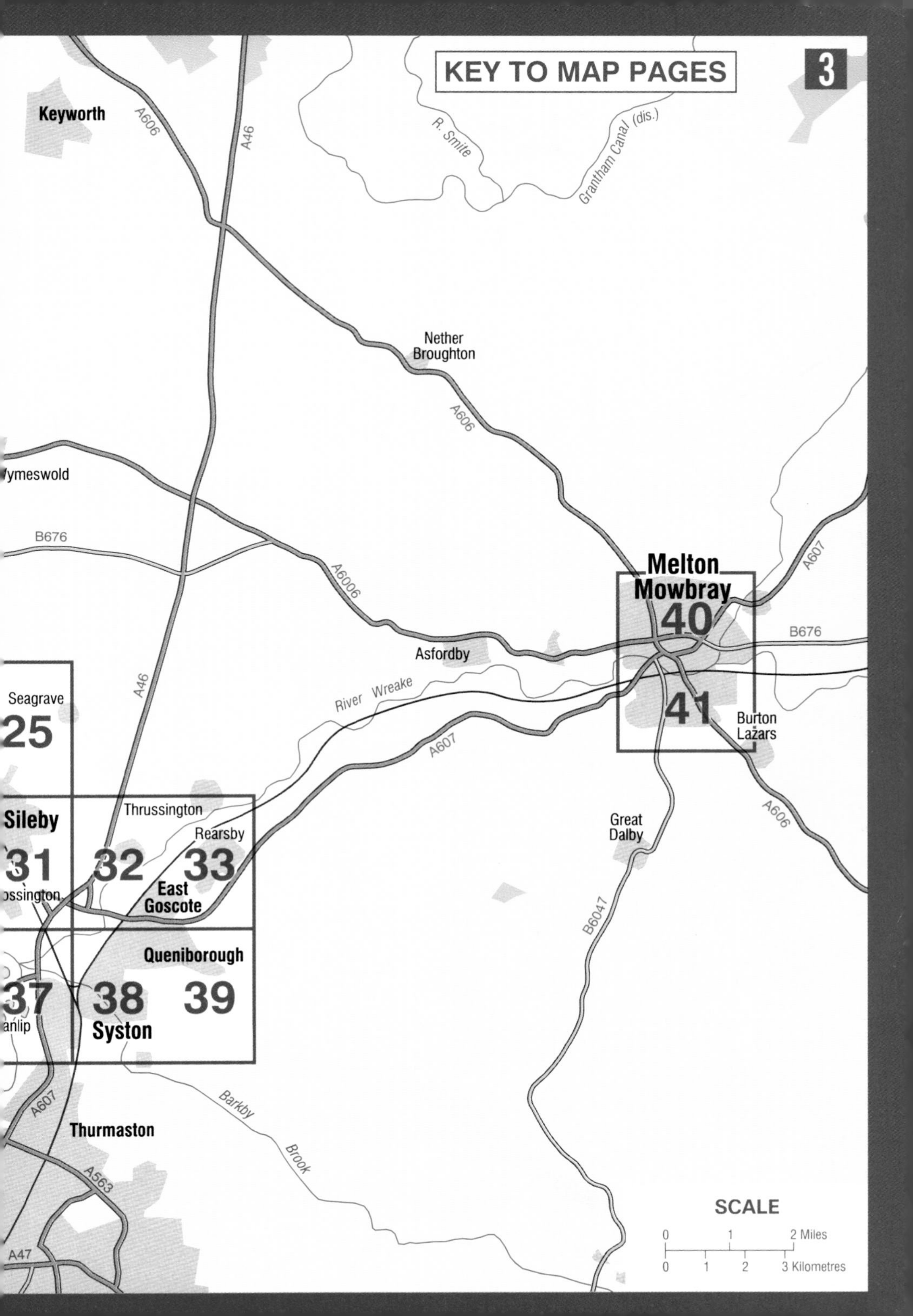

Keyworth

A606

A46

R. Smite

Grantham Canal (dis.)

Nether Broughton

A606

Wymeswold

B676

A6006

A46

Melton Mowbray

40

A607

B676

Asfordby

River Wreake

A607

Seagrave

25

Sileby

31

ossington

Thrussington

Rearsby

32 **33**

East Goscote

41

Burton Lazars

Great Dalby

A606

B6047

Queniborough

37 **38** **39**

anlip

Syston

Barkby

Brook

A607

Thurmaston

A563

A47

SCALE

0   1   2 Miles

0   1   2   3 Kilometres

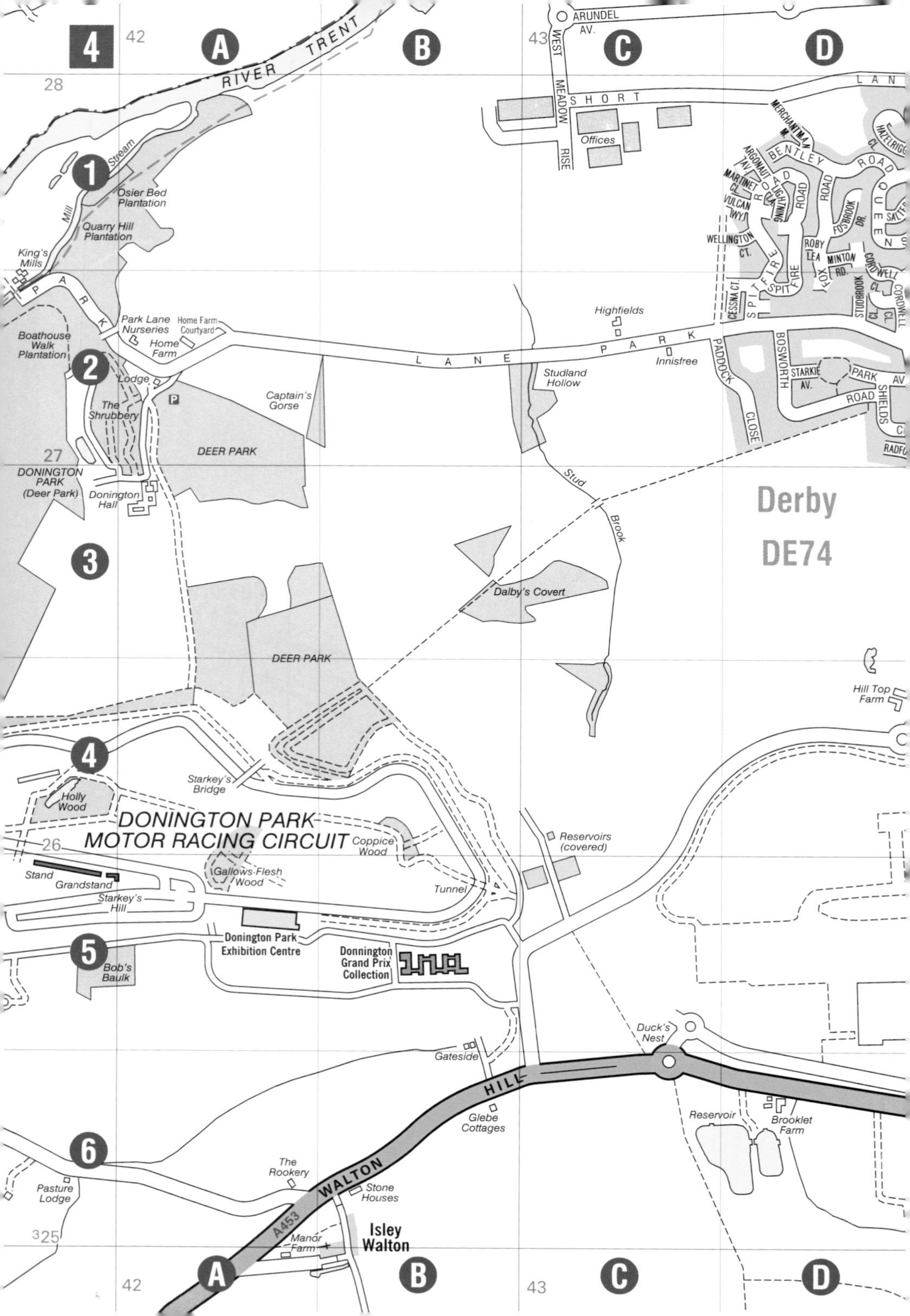
A
B
C
D
1
2
3
4
5
6
42
43
28
27
26
325
RIVER TRENT
ARUNDEL AV.
WEST MEADOW RISE
SHORT LANE
Offices
MERCHANTMAN M.
BENTLEY ROAD
ARGONAUT AV.
MARTINET CL.
VULCAN WY.
LIGHTNING
ROAD
WELLINGTON CT.
SPITFIRE
CESSNA CT.
ROBY LEA
FOX
MINTON RD.
FOSBROOK DR.
QUEENS
HAZELRIGG
CL.
CORDWELL CL.
STUDBROOK CL.
CORDWELL CL.
Stream
Mill
Osier Bed Plantation
Quarry Hill Plantation
King's Mills
PARK LANE
Park Lane Nurseries
Home Farm Courtyard
Home Farm
Highfields
Innisfree
PADDOCK CLOSE
BOSWORTH
STARKIE AV.
PARK ROAD
SHIELDS
AV
RADFO
Boathouse Walk Plantation
Lodge
P
The Shrubbery
Captain's Gorse
Studland Hollow
DEER PARK
DONINGTON PARK (Deer Park)
Donington Hall
Stud Brook
Derby
DE74
Dalby's Covert
DEER PARK
Hill Top Farm
Starkey's Bridge
Holly Wood
DONINGTON PARK MOTOR RACING CIRCUIT
Coppice Wood
Reservoirs (covered)
Stand
Grandstand
Gallows Flesh Wood
Starkey's Hill
Tunnel
Donington Park Exhibition Centre
Donnington Grand Prix Collection
Bob's Baulk
Duck's Nest
Gateside
HILL
Glebe Cottages
Reservoir
Brooklet Farm
The Rookery
WALTON
A453
Stone Houses
Pasture Lodge
Manor Farm
Isley Walton

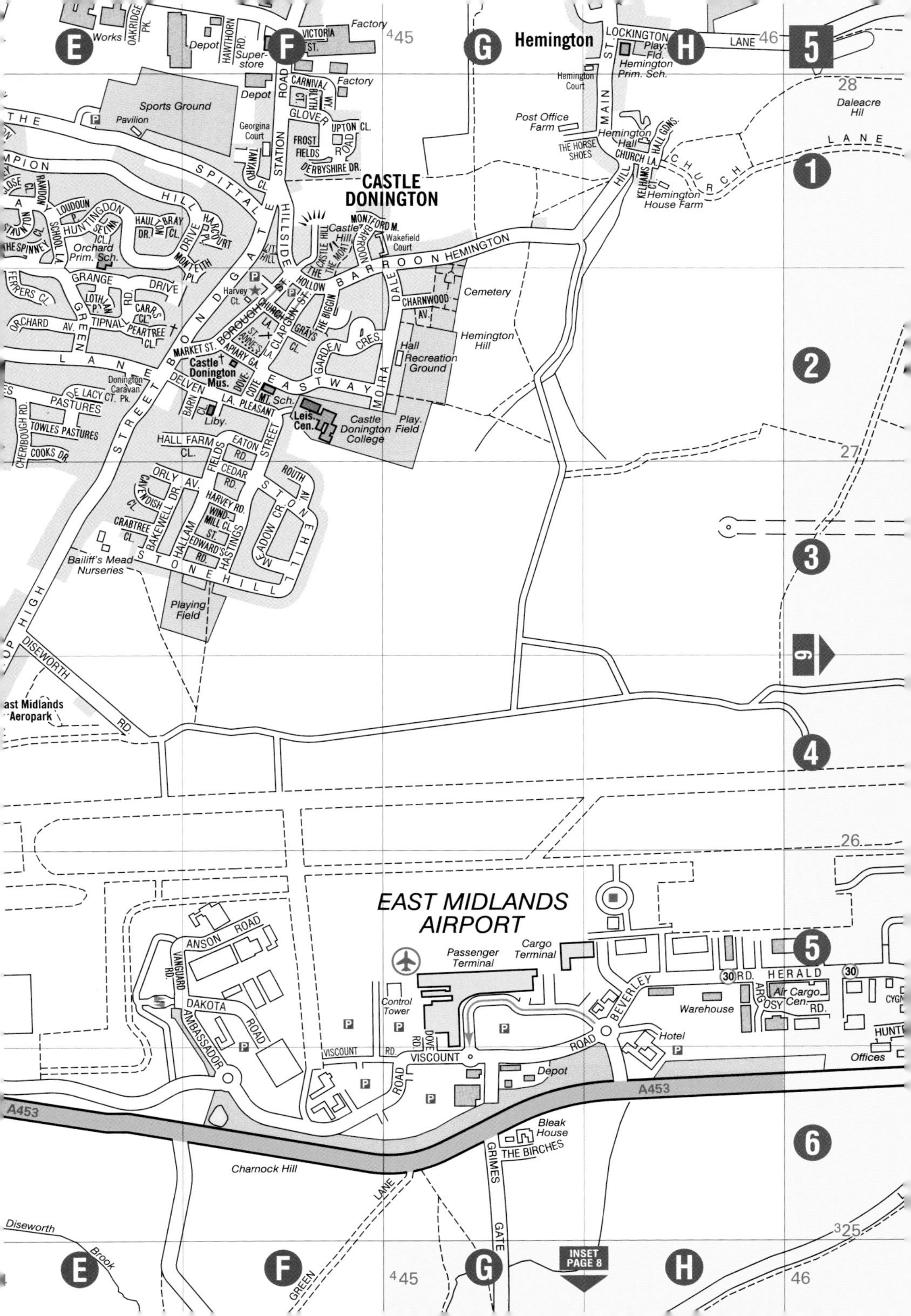

E
F
G
H
5
445
46
Hemington
Works
OAKRIDGE PK.
Depot
HAWTHORN RD.
Superstore
VICTORIA ST.
Factory
LOCKINGTON
LANE
Play. Fld.
Hemington Prim. Sch.
Hemington Court
28
Daleacre Hil
Sports Ground
Pavilion
Depot
CARNIVAL
BLYTH CT.
WY.
Factory
GLOVER
UPTON CL.
Georgina Court
FROST FIELDS
ROAD
DERBYSHIRE DR.
TANYARD CL.
STATION ROAD
Post Office Farm
MAIN ST.
Hemington Hall
HALL GDNS.
THE HORSE SHOES
CHURCH LA.
CHURCH LANE
1
THE SPITTAL
HILL
KELHAMS CT.
Hemington House Farm
CASTLE DONINGTON
HILLSIDE
RAWDON
LOUDOUN P.
HUNTINGDON
SELINA CL.
HAULTON DR.
BRAY CL.
HARCOURT
DRIVE
STAUNTON CL.
SCHOOL LA.
THE SPINNEY
Orchard Prim. Sch.
MONTEITH PL.
Castle Hill
MONTFORD M.
BARROON
Wakefield Court
THE CASTLE HILL
THE MOAT
LITTLE HILL
BARROON
HEMINGTON
THE HOLLOW
GRANGE
DRIVE
FERRERS CL.
LOTHIAN P.
RD.
CARRS CL.
Harvey Ct.
BONDGATE
ST.
CHURCH
BOROUGH
CLAPGUN ST.
THE BIGGIN
DALE
CHARNWOOD AV.
Cemetery
ORCHARD AV.
TIPNALL
PEARTREE CL.
GREEN LANE
MARKET ST.
ST. ANNE'S LA.
APIARY GA.
GRAYS CL.
GARDEN CRES.
Hemington Hill
Castle Donington Mus.
DOVECOTE
Donington Caravan Pk.
EASTWAY
MOIRA
Hall
Recreation Ground
2
DE LACY CT.
PASTURES
DELVEN LA.
BARN CL.
Liby.
PLEASANT
MT. Sch.
Leis. Cen.
Castle Donington College
Play. Field
CHERIBOUGH RD.
TOWLES PASTURES
COOKS DR.
STREET
HALL FARM CL.
EATON RD.
STREET
27
ORLY AV.
FIELDS
CEDAR RD.
ROUTH AV.
CAVENDISH CL.
BAKEWELL DR.
HARVEY RD.
STONEHILL
CRABTREE CL.
HALLAM
WINDMILL CL.
EDWARD'S RD.
HASTINGS ST.
MEADOW CR.
3
Bailiff's Mead Nurseries
STONEHILL
Playing Field
TOP HIGH
DISEWORTH RD.
9
East Midlands Aeropark
4
26
EAST MIDLANDS AIRPORT
ANSON ROAD
Cargo Terminal
Passenger Terminal
5
VANGUARD RD.
30
RD.
HERALD
30
DAKOTA ROAD
Control Tower
BEVERLEY
ARGOSY RD.
Air Cargo Cen.
Warehouse
CYGN
AMBASSADOR
DOVE RD.
ROAD
Hotel
HUNT
VISCOUNT RD.
VISCOUNT
Depot
Offices
ROAD
A453
A453
Bleak House
THE BIRCHES
6
Charnock Hill
GRIMES GATE
LANE
Diseworth
Brook
GREEN
INSET PAGE 8
325
E
F
445
G
H
46

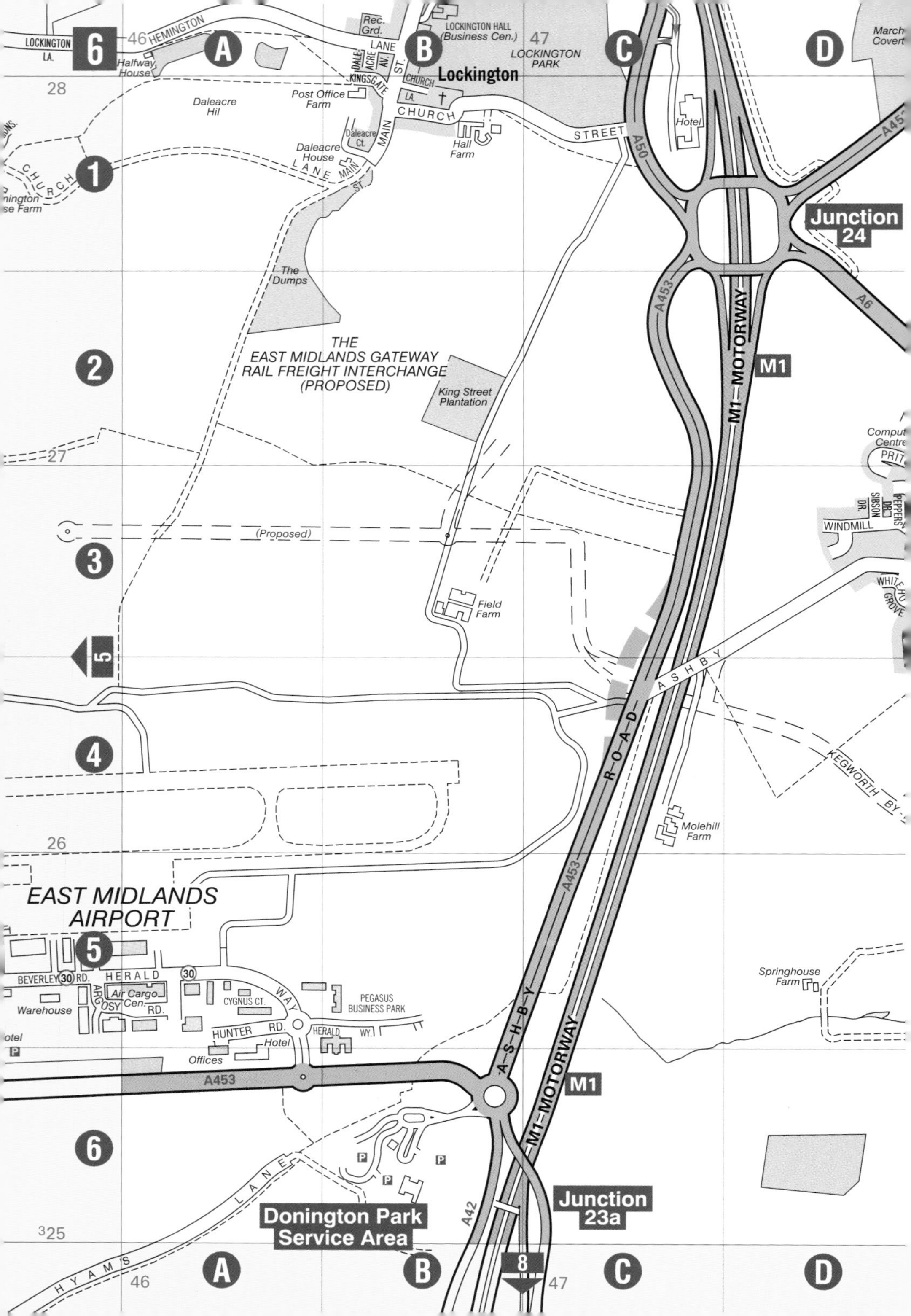
LOCKINGTON LA.
6
46
HEMINGTON
LANE
Halfway House
Rec. Grd.
LOCKINGTON HALL (Business Cen.)
47
LOCKINGTON PARK
Lockington
March Covert
28
Daleacre Hil
Post Office Farm
DALE-ACRE AV.
KINGSGATE
CHURCH
LA.
CHURCH STREET
Hall Farm
Hotel
Daleacre Ct.
Daleacre House
MAIN ST.
LANE
CHURCH
A50
A453
A6
Junction 24
The Dumps
THE EAST MIDLANDS GATEWAY RAIL FREIGHT INTERCHANGE (PROPOSED)
King Street Plantation
M1 MOTORWAY
M1
27
(Proposed)
Field Farm
WINDMILL
SIBSON DR.
PEPPERS DR.
WHITEHILL GROVE
5
ASHBY ROAD
KEGWORTH BY
Molehill Farm
26
EAST MIDLANDS AIRPORT
BEVERLEY RD.
HERALD WAY
30
ARGOSY RD.
Air Cargo Cen.
CYGNUS CT.
PEGASUS BUSINESS PARK
Warehouse
HUNTER RD.
HERALD WY.
Hotel
Offices
A453
ASHBY
Springhouse Farm
M1
M1 MOTORWAY
LANE
HYAMS
Donington Park Service Area
A42
Junction 23a
325
46
8
47
A B C D
1 2 3 4 5 6

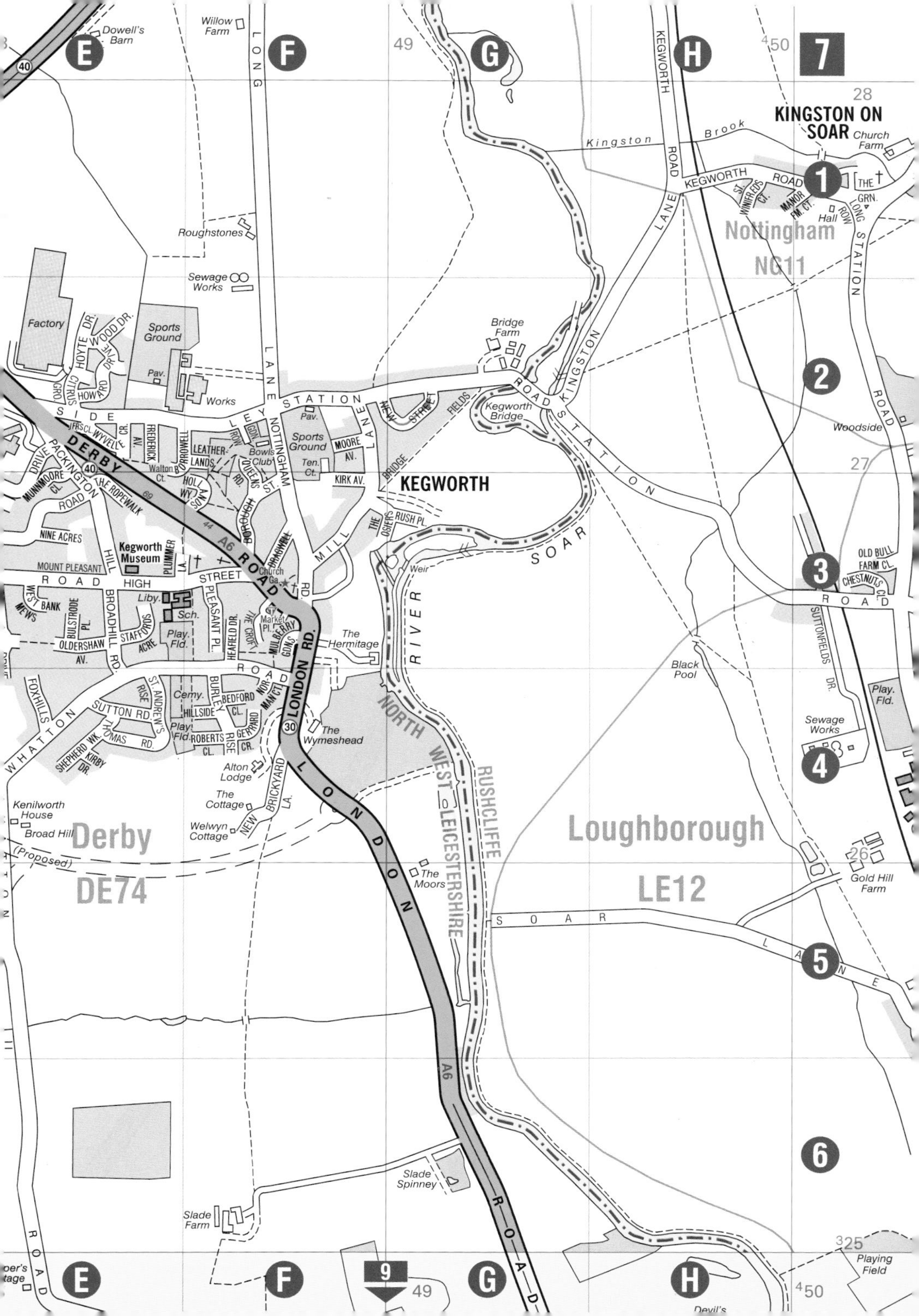

Dowell's Barn

Willow Farm

LONG LANE

Roughstones

Sewage Works

Factory

HOYLE DR.
WOOD DR.
CRIS.
HOW AV.

Sports Ground

Pav.

Works

LEY NOTTINGHAM LANE

STATION

Pav.

NEW ST.

FIELDS

Bridge Farm

Kegworth Bridge

ROAD

KINGSTON

STATION

ROAD

KINGSTON ON SOAR
Church Farm

KEGWORTH ROAD

ST. WINIFRED'S PL.
MANOR FM. CT.
Hall

LONG STATION ROW

THE GRN.

1

Nottingham

NG11

28

2

Woodside

27

DERBY

40

A44

A6

PACKINGTON CL.
DRIVE
MUNNMOORE CL.
HISCL.
WYVELL CR.
FREDERICK AV.
CROWELL
Walton St.
QUEENS RD.
HOL. WY.
AMOS RD.
BRANDHILL
LEATHER-LANDS
Bowls Club
Sports Ground
Ten. Ct.
MOORE AV.
KIRK AV.

KEGWORTH

THE JOFFS
RUSH PL.

RIVER

SOAR

Weir

3

OLD BULL FARM CL.
CHESTNUTS

ROAD

SUTTONFIELDS DR.

Play. Fld.

Sewage Works

4

Nine Acres
MOUNT PLEASANT
ROAD
WEST BANK
MEWS
BULSTRODE PL.
OLDERSHAW AV.
BROADHILL RD.
FOXHILLS
HILL
HIGH
Kegworth Museum
PLUMMER
Liby.
Sch.
Play. Fld.
STAFFORDS
ACRS.
PLEASANT PL.
HEAFIELD DR.
BURR OAK
NOR MANT GDNS.
MILBERRY GDNS.
Market Pl.
STREET
Church
LONDON RD.
ROAD
MILL LANE
BRIDGE
THE
The Hermitage
30
The Wymeshead
Black Pool

WHATTON
SUTTON AV.
S. ANDREW'S RISE
THOMAS RD.
SHEPHERD WY.
KIRBY DR.
HILLSIDE
Play Fld
BEDFORD CL.
RISE
ROBERTS CL.
GERVARD
CR.
ALTON Lodge
Alton Lodge
BRICKYARD LA.
NEW
The Cottage

Kenilworth House
Broad Hill

Derby

(Proposed)

DE74

Welwyn Cottage

The Moors

NORTH WEST LEICESTERSHIRE

RUSHCLIFFE

LONDON

ROAD

SOAR

Loughborough

LE12

LANE

5

26

Gold Hill Farm

6

Slade Spinney

A6

Slade Farm

per's tage

325

Playing Field

Devil's

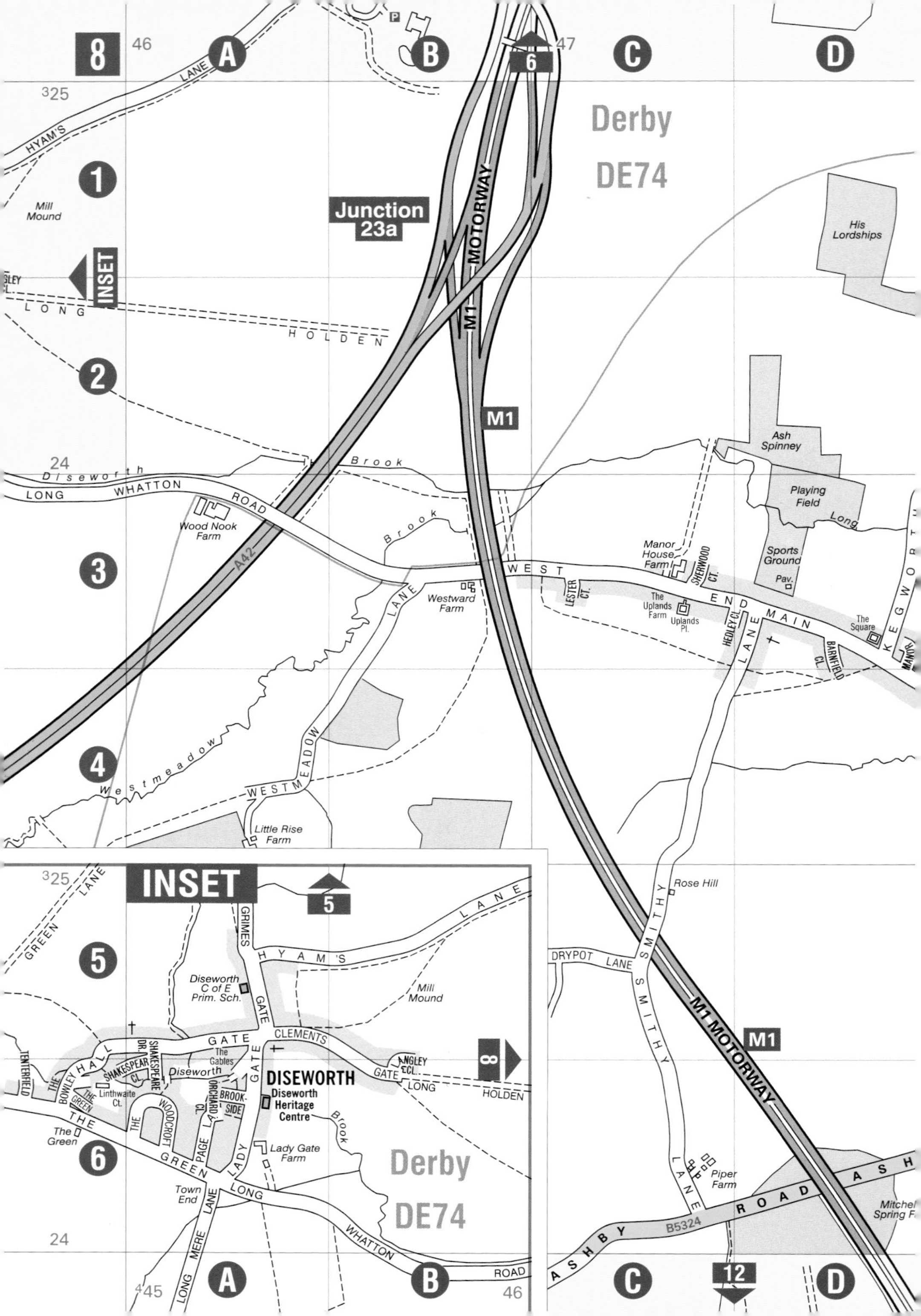

8
46
A
B
47
C
D
6
325
Derby
DE74
HYAM'S
LANE
Mill
Mound
Junction
23a
M1 MOTORWAY
INSET
LONG
HOLDEN
His
Lordships
M1
24
Diseworth
Brook
LONG WHATTON ROAD
Wood Nook
Farm
A42
Ash
Spinney
Playing
Field
Long
Manor
House
Farm
SHERWOOD CT.
Sports
Ground
Pav.
WEST END MAIN
LESTER CT.
The
Uplands
Farm
Uplands
Pl.
HEDLEY CL.
LANE
BARNFIELD CL.
The
Square
KEGWORTH
MANOR
Westward
Farm
LANE
WESTMEADOW
Westmeadow
Little Rise
Farm
Rose Hill
SMITHY
DRYPOT LANE
M1 MOTORWAY
M1
Piper
Farm
ASHBY ROAD
B5324
ASH
Mitchel
Spring F
12
INSET
5
GREEN LANE
GRIMES GATE
HYAM'S LANE
Diseworth
C of E
Prim. Sch.
Mill
Mound
TENTERFIELD
HALL GATE
CLEMENTS GATE
ANGLEY CL.
LONG HOLDEN
DR.
SHAKESPEARE
The
Gables
Diseworth
SHAKESPEAR CL.
THE BOWLEY
THE GREEN
Linthwaite
Ct.
THE WOODCROFT
ORCHARD CL.
BROOK-SIDE
DISEWORTH
Diseworth
Heritage
Centre
Brook
THE GREEN
The
Green
PAGE LA
LADY GATE
Lady Gate
Farm
Town
End
LONG WHATTON ROAD
LONG MERE LANE
445
46

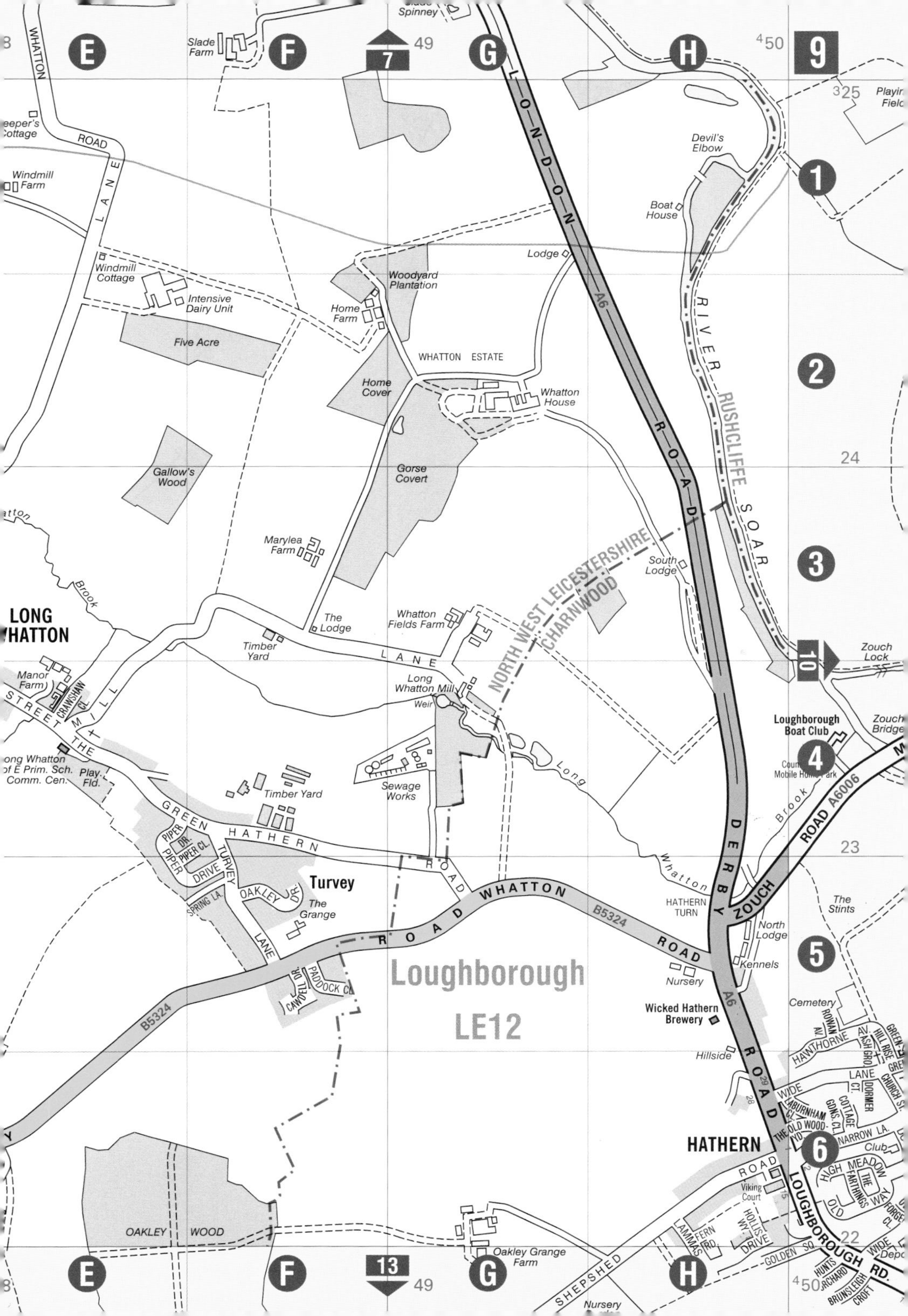

9
E
F
G
H
7
49
450
325
13
Slade Farm
Spinney
WHATTON ROAD LANE
Keeper's Cottage
Windmill Farm
Windmill Cottage
Intensive Dairy Unit
Five Acre
Gallow's Wood
Woodyard Plantation
Home Farm
WHATTON ESTATE
Home Cover
Whatton House
Gorse Covert
Lodge
LONDON ROAD
A6
Devil's Elbow
Boat House
RIVER SOAR
RUSHCLIFFE
NORTH WEST LEICESTERSHIRE
CHARNWOOD
South Lodge
Marylea Farm
Brook
LONG WHATTON
The Lodge
Timber Yard
Whatton Fields Farm
LANE
Zouch Lock
10
Manor Farm
CRAWSHAW CL.
THE STREET
MILL
Long Whatton Mill
Weir
Long Whatton C of E Prim. Sch. Comm. Cen.
Play. Fld.
Timber Yard
Sewage Works
Long
Loughborough Boat Club
Zouch Bridge
Mobile Home Park
Brook
ROAD A6006
GREEN HATHERN ROAD
PIPER DR.
PIPER CL.
PIPER DRIVE
TURVEY
Turvey
OAKLEY DR.
The Grange
SPRING LA.
LANE
WHATTON ROAD
B5324
Whatton
HATHERN TURN
DERBY ROAD
ZOUCH
North Lodge
Kennels
Nursery
The Stints
Loughborough
LE12
PADDOCK CL.
CAWDELL DR.
B5324
Wicked Hathern Brewery
Cemetery
ROWAN AV.
HAWTHORNE AV.
ASH GRO.
HILL RISE
Hillside
LANE
WIDE
CT.
DORMER
CHURCH ST.
LABURNHAM
COTTAGE GDNS. CL.
THE OLD WOOD-YD.
NARROW LA.
Club
HATHERN
HIGH MEADOW WAY
THE FARTHINGS
OLD FORGE CL.
ROAD
Viking Court
LOUGHBOROUGH RD.
OAKLEY WOOD
Oakley Grange Farm
SHEPSHED
Nursery
LAMMAS
FERN RD.
HOLLIS WY.
DRIVE
GOLDEN SQ.
HUNTS ORCHARD
BRUNSLEIGH CROFT
WIDE
Depot
22
23
24
1
2
3
4
5
6

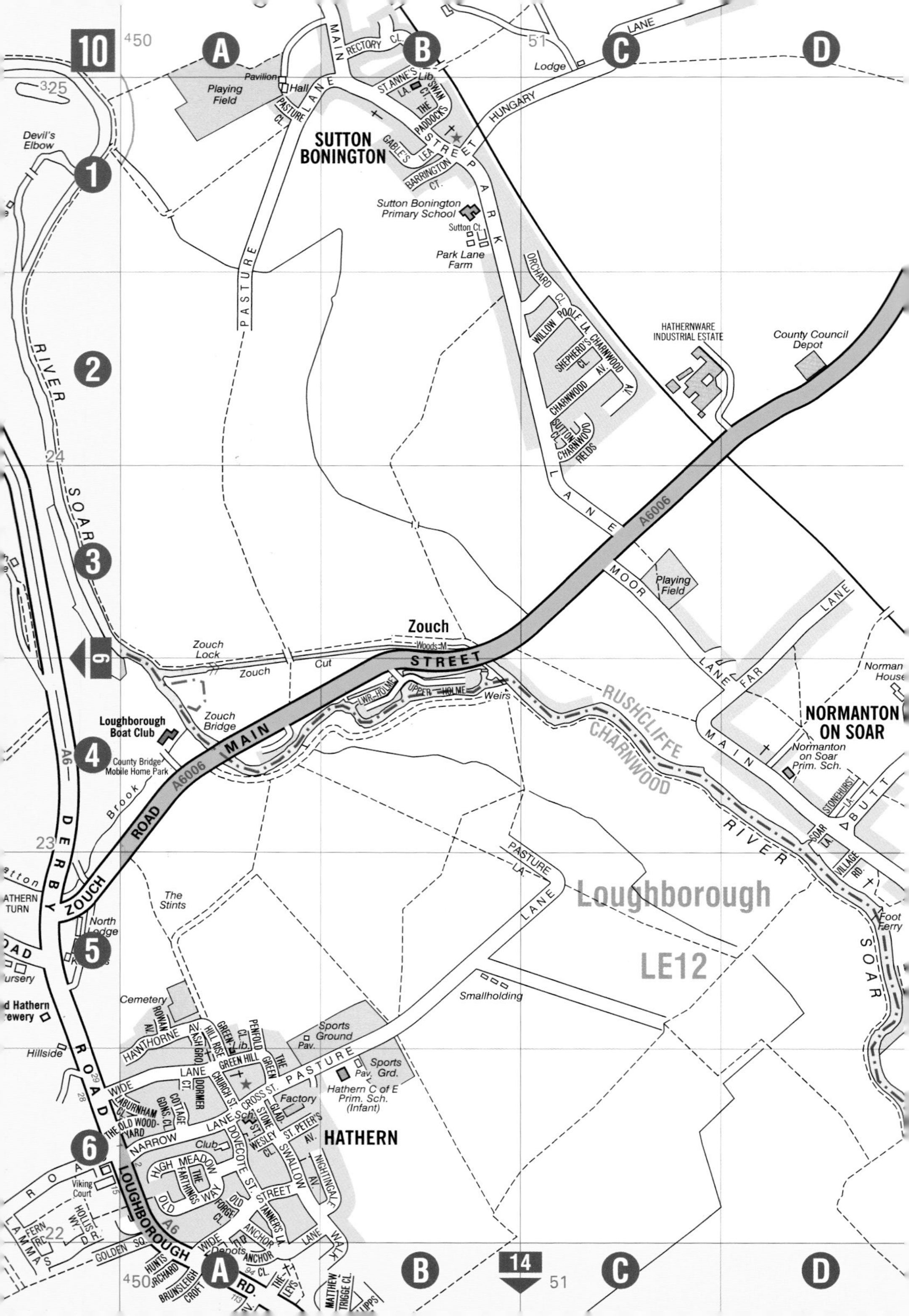
SUTTON BONINGTON
Playing Field
Pavilion
Hall
Sutton Bonington Primary School
Sutton Ct.
Park Lane Farm
HATHERNWARE INDUSTRIAL ESTATE
County Council Depot
Devil's Elbow
RIVER SOAR
Zouch
Zouch Lock
Zouch Cut
Zouch Bridge
Woods M
Weirs
Loughborough Boat Club
County Bridge Mobile Home Park
MAIN STREET
MAIN ROAD
A6006
ZOUCH ROAD
DERBY ROAD
LOUGHBOROUGH ROAD
A6
RUSHCLIFFE
CHARNWOOD
NORMANTON ON SOAR
Normanton on Soar Prim. Sch.
Norman House
Foot Ferry
MOOR LANE
FAR LANE
MAIN STREET
Playing Field
The Stints
North Lodge
Cemetery
Loughborough
LE12
Smallholding
Sports Ground
Pav.
Sports Grd.
Hathern C of E Prim. Sch. (Infant)
Factory
Club
HATHERN
Viking Court
Depots
Hillside
Hathern Brewery
PASTURE LANE
HUNGARY LANE
Lodge
Lib.

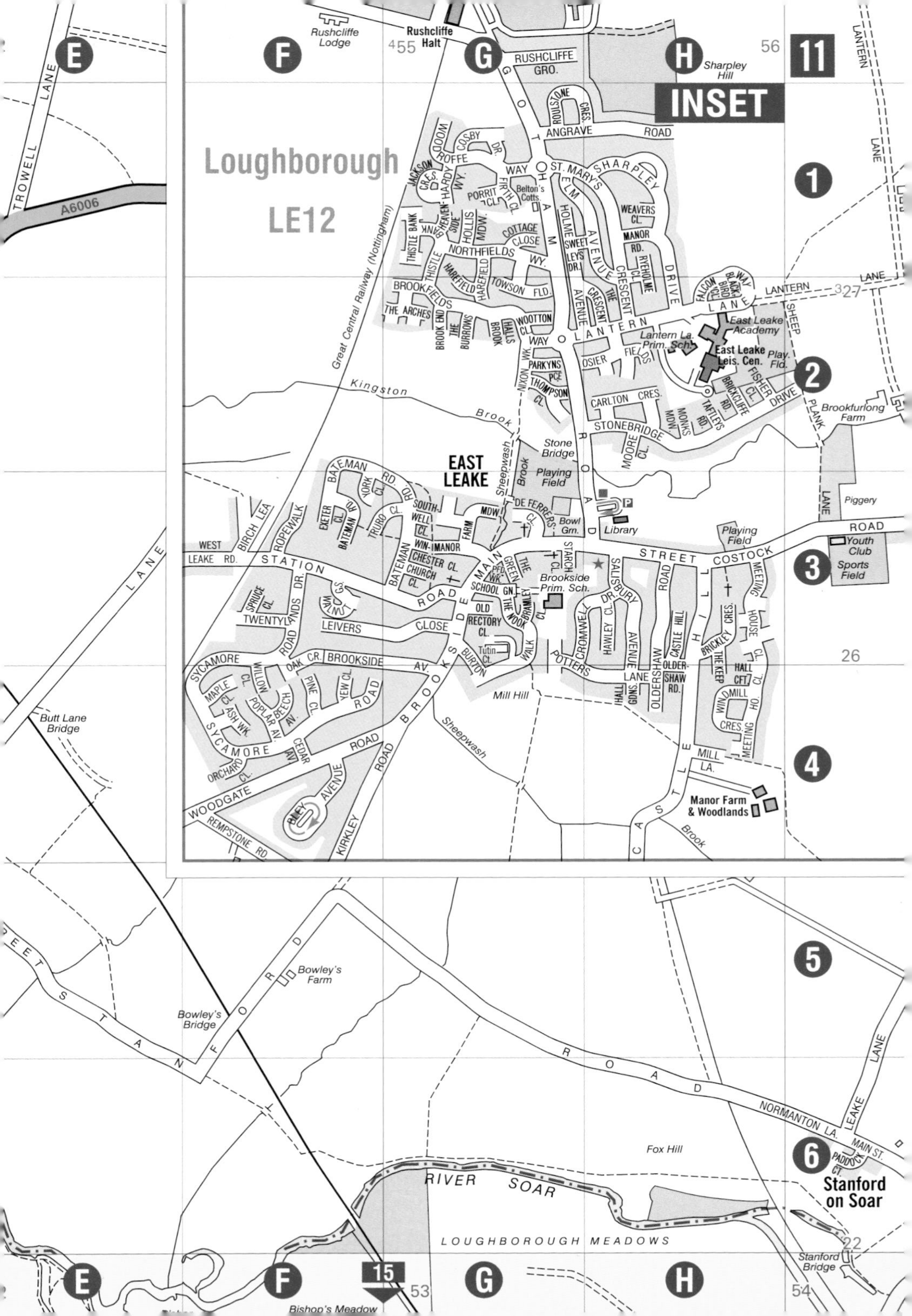
11
INSET
Loughborough
LE12
EAST LEAKE
Stanford on Soar
Rushcliffe Lodge
Rushcliffe Halt
Sharpley Hill
RUSHCLIFFE GRO.
ROULSTONE CRES.
ANGRAVE ROAD
GOTHAM ROAD
ST. MARY'S
SHARPLEY DRIVE
WEAVERS CL.
MANOR RD.
RYEHOLME CL.
ELM AVENUE
HOLME
SWEET LEYS DR.
THE CRESCENT
CRESCENT AVENUE
FALCON WAY
BLACKBIRD CL.
LANTERN LANE
East Leake Academy
Lantern La. Prim. Sch.
East Leake Leis. Cen.
Play. Fld.
SHEEP PLANK LANE
FISHER CL.
DRIVE
BRICKCLIFFE RD.
TAFTLEYS RD.
MONKS MDW.
OSIER FIELDS
CARLTON CRES.
STONEBRIDGE
MOORE CL.
Brookfurlong Farm
Piggery
COSBY DR.
WOOD ROFFE WAY
JACKSON CRES.
HARDY WY.
PORRIT CL.
FIRTH CL.
Belton's Cotts.
THISTLE BANK
BHENEVEN SIDE
HOLLIS MDW.
COTTAGE CLOSE WY.
NORTHFIELDS
HAREFIELD
TOWSON FLD.
BROOKFIELDS
THE ARCHES
BROOK END
THE BURROWS
BROOK
HALLS
WOOTTON CL.
WAY
NIXON WK.
PARKYNS PCE
THOMPSON CL.
Kingston Brook
Great Central Railway (Nottingham)
Stone Bridge
Playing Field
Sheepwash Brook
BATEMAN RD.
YORK CL.
EXETER CL.
TRURO CL.
SOUTHWELL CL.
WIN-IMANOR
CHESTER CL.
CHURCH CL.
FARM MDW
DE FERRERS CL.
Bowl Grn.
Library
WEST LEAKE RD.
BIRCH LEA
ROPEWALK
STATION ROAD
MAIN STREET
SPRUCE CL.
WALNUT GS.
TWENTYLANDS DR.
LEIVERS CLOSE
PFD WK.
THE GREEN
SCHOOL GN.
OLD RECTORY CL.
THE NOOK
BRAMLEY CL.
WALK
Brookside Prim. Sch.
STARCH CL.
COSTOCK ROAD
Playing Field
Youth Club
Sports Field
SALISBURY DR.
CROMWELL
HAWLEY CL.
AVENUE
ROAD
CASTLE HILL
BRICKLEY CRES.
MEETING HOUSE CL.
THE KEEP
HALL CFT.
OLDERSHAW RD.
POTTERS LANE
HALL GDNS.
WINDMILL CRES.
MEETING HO. CL.
MILL LA.
Tutin Ct.
BURTON
BROOKSIDE
SYCAMORE ROAD
OAK CR.
BROOKSIDE AV.
MAPLE CL.
WILLOW CL.
ASH WK.
POPLAR AV.
BEECH AV.
PINE CL.
YEW CL.
ORCHARD CL.
CEDAR AV.
WOODGATE ROAD
REMPSTONE RD.
BAILEY
AVENUE
KIRKLEY ROAD
Mill Hill
Sheepwash
Manor Farm & Woodlands
Brook
CASTLE HILL
TROWELL LANE
A6006
LANE
Butt Lane Bridge
STANFORD ROAD
Bowley's Farm
Bowley's Bridge
NORMANTON LA.
LEAKE LANE
MAIN ST.
PADDOCK CT.
Fox Hill
RIVER SOAR
LOUGHBOROUGH MEADOWS
Stanford Bridge
Bishop's Meadow
LANTERN LANE
E F G H
1 2 3 4 5 6
455 56 53 54
327 26 22
15

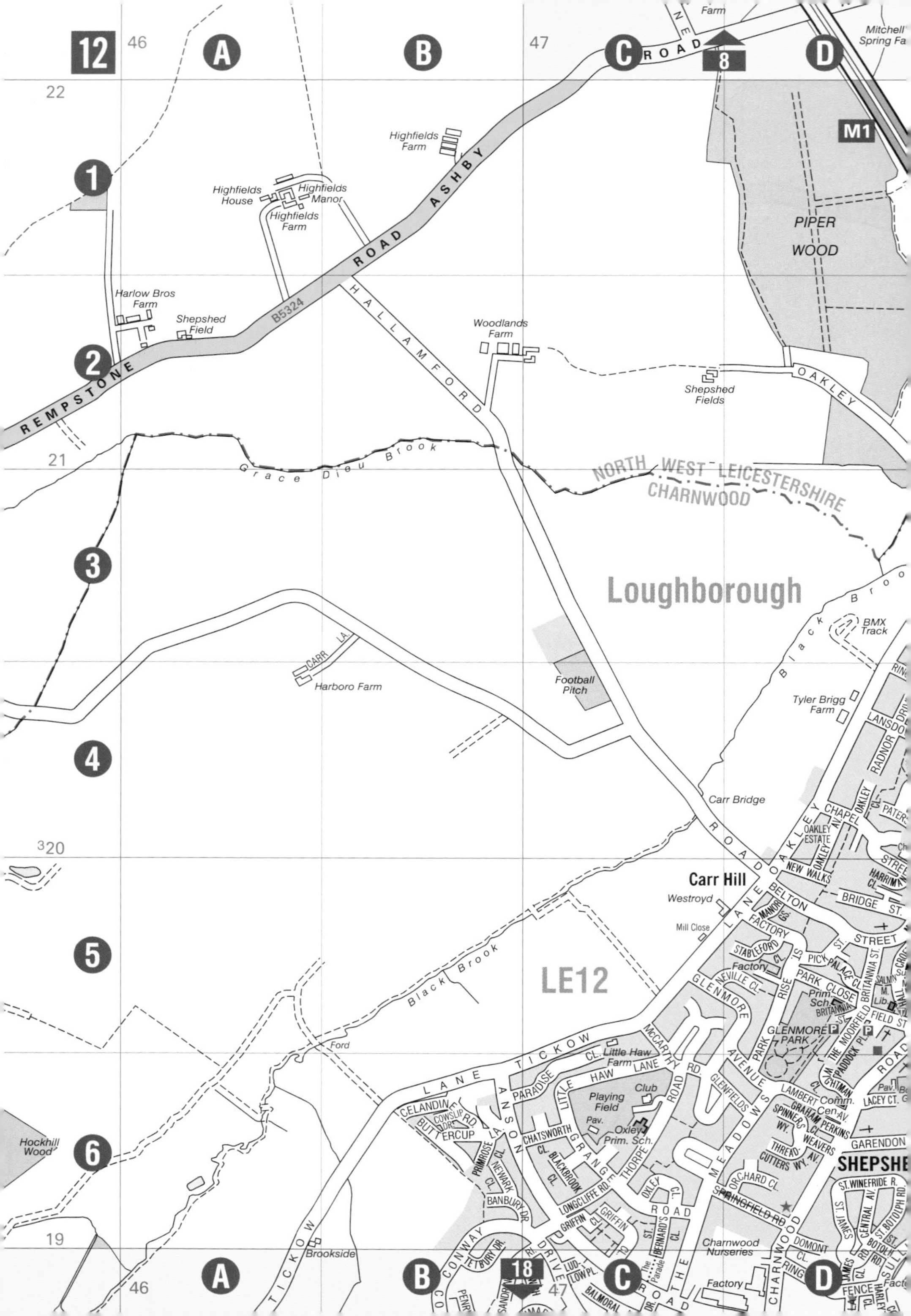

A
B
C
D
46
47
22
21
20
19
1
2
3
4
5
6
8
18
M1
ROAD
ASHBY ROAD
B5324
REMPSTONE
HALLAMFORD ROAD
OAKLEY
Highfields Farm
Highfields House
Highfields Manor
Highfields Farm
Harlow Bros Farm
Shepshed Field
Woodlands Farm
Shepshed Fields
PIPER WOOD
Mitchell's Spring Farm
Grace Dieu Brook
NORTH WEST LEICESTERSHIRE
CHARNWOOD
Loughborough
Black Brook
BMX Track
CARR LA.
Harboro Farm
Football Pitch
Tyler Brigg Farm
Carr Bridge
Carr Hill
Westroyd
Mill Close
LE12
Black Brook
Ford
TICKOW LANE
Little Haw Farm
Playing Field
Club
Pav.
Oxley Prim. Sch.
Hockhill Wood
Brookside
Charnwood Nurseries
Factory
SHEPSHED

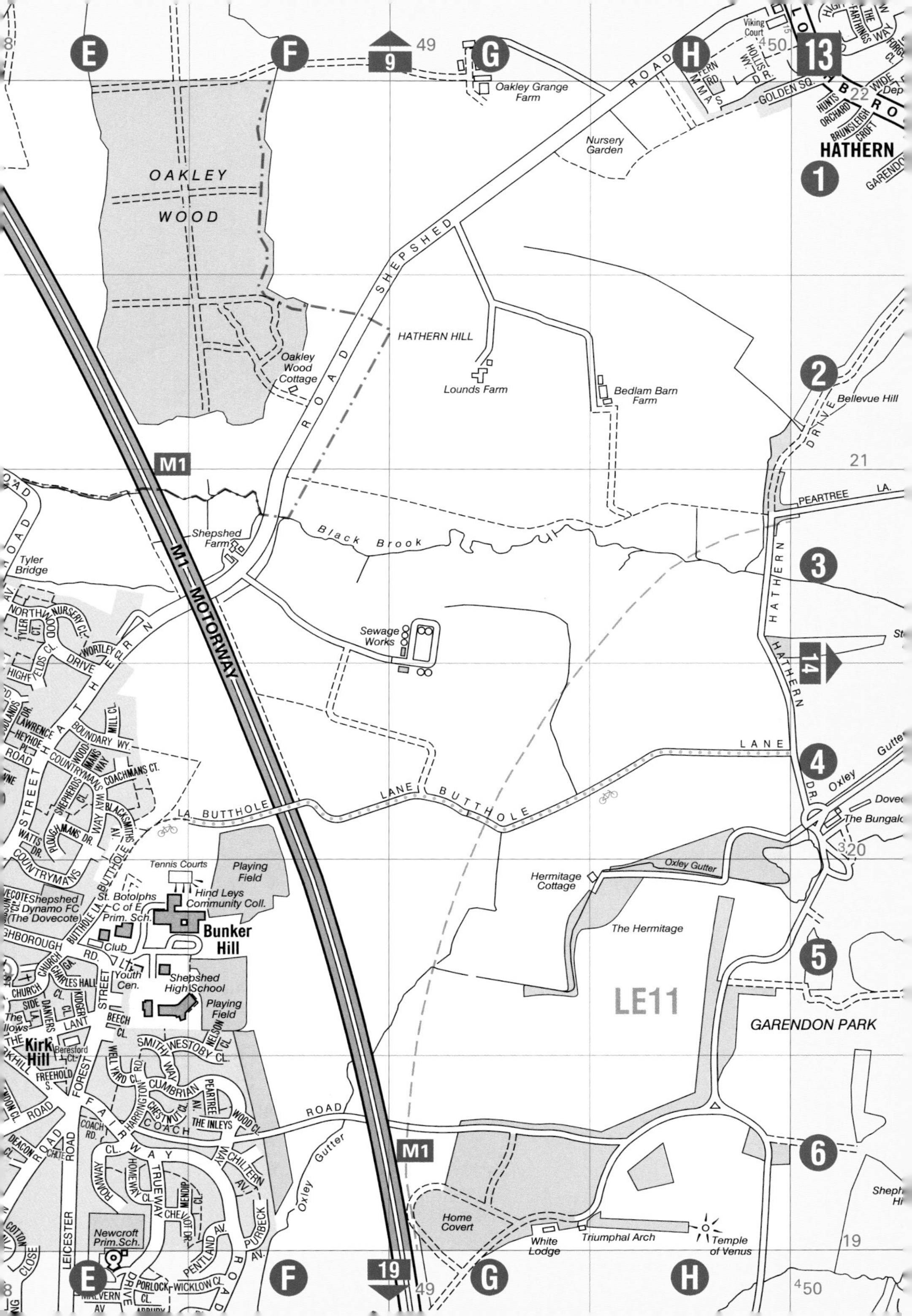

13
9
14
19
E
F
G
H
1
2
3
4
5
6
49
450
21
320
19
HATHERN
OAKLEY WOOD
Oakley Grange Farm
Oakley Wood Cottage
Nursery Garden
HATHERN HILL
Lounds Farm
Bedlam Barn Farm
Bellevue Hill
SHEPSHED ROAD
PEARTREE LA.
HATHERN DRIVE
Black Brook
Shepshed Farm
Tyler Bridge
M1
M1 MOTORWAY
Sewage Works
BUTTHOLE LANE
LANE
Oxley Gutter
Oxley DR.
The Bungalow
Hermitage Cottage
The Hermitage
LE11
GARENDON PARK
Tennis Courts
Playing Field
Hind Leys Community Coll.
Bunker Hill
St. Botolphs C of E Prim. Sch.
Club
Youth Cen.
Shepshed High School
Kirk Hill
Shepshed Dynamo FC (The Dovecote)
ROAD
Home Covert
White Lodge
Triumphal Arch
Temple of Venus
Newcroft Prim.Sch.
LEICESTER ROAD
FOREST STREET
CHURCH ST.
COACH WAY
FAIR WAY
HATHERN DRIVE
COUNTRYMANS WAY
BOUNDARY WY.
COACHMANS CT.
WORTLEY CL.
NURSERY CL.
PENTLAND AV.
WICKLOW CL.
PORLOCK
MALVERN AV.
CUMBRIAN WAY
THE INLEYS
WOOD CL.
CHILTERN AV.
PURBECK AV.
MENDIP CL.
CHEVIOT DR.
TRUEWAY
HOMEWAY CL.
ROMWAY
GOLDEN SQ.
HUNTS ORCHARD
BRUNSLEIGH CROFT
Viking Court
HOLLIS DR.
FERN RD.

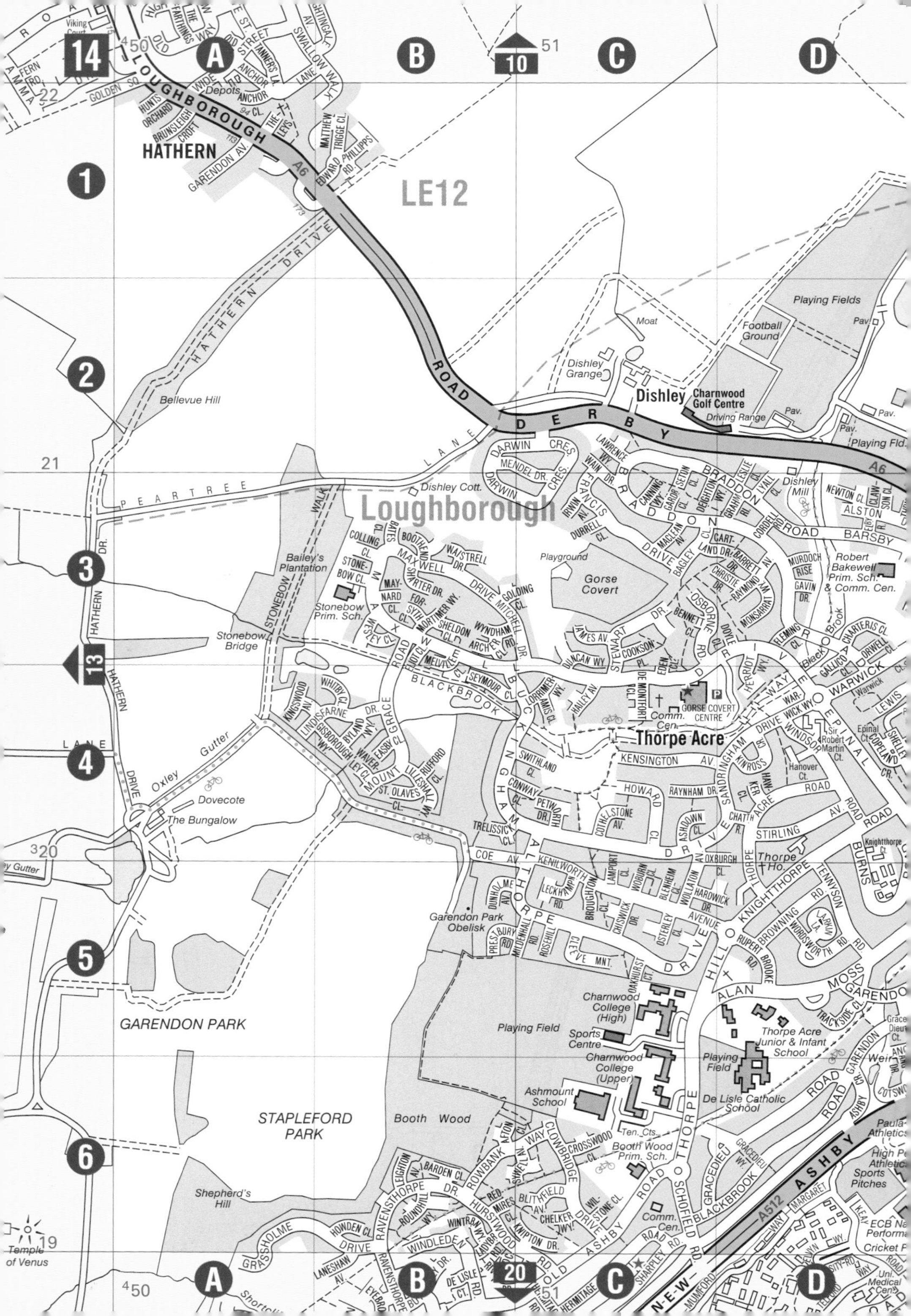
14
10
20
13
A
B
C
D
1
2
3
4
5
6
450
51
22
21
320
19
HATHERN
LE12
Loughborough
Dishley
Thorpe Acre
LOUGHBOROUGH ROAD
DERBY ROAD
A6
A512
ASHBY ROAD
HATHERN DRIVE
PEARTREE LANE
HATHERN LANE
Viking Court
Depots
GOLDEN SQ.
HUNTS
ORCHARD
BRUNSLEIGH
CROFT
GARENDON AV.
WIDE
ANCHOR
ANCHOR CL.
OLD WAY
OLD STREET
TANNER'S LA.
SWALLOW WALK
LANE
THE LEYS
MATTHEW
TRIGGE CL.
EDWARD RD.
PHILLIPPS
Bellevue Hill
Moat
Dishley Grange
Charnwood Golf Centre
Driving Range
Football Ground
Playing Fields
Pav.
Playing Fld.
Dishley Mill
Dishley Cott.
DARWIN CRES.
MENDEL DR.
LAWRENCE WY.
FRANCIS DR.
WAIN DR.
IRWIN AV.
DURRELL CL.
BRADDON DRIVE
BRADDON ROAD
CANNING WY.
GARDR CL.
SETON CL.
DEIGHTON WY.
GRAHAM RI.
LESLIE CL.
LYALL CL.
CORDELL RD.
NEWTON CL.
CLAWSON CL.
ALSTON
BARSBY
MACLEAN AV.
BAGLEY CL.
CARTLAND DR.
BARRETT DR.
CHRISTIE DR.
RAYMOND AV.
MONSARRAT WY.
MURDOCH RISE
GAVIN DR.
Robert Bakewell Prim. Sch. & Comm. Cen.
Playground
Gorse Covert
Bailey's Plantation
STONEBOW WALK
COLLING CL.
BATES CL.
BOOTHE CL.
MAXWELL DRIVE
WALSTRELL DR.
STONEBOW CL.
MAYNARD CL.
FORSYTH CL.
SHARTER DR.
MORTIMER WY.
SHELDON CL.
WYNDHAM RD.
ARCHER CL.
MITCHELL DR.
GOLDING CL.
Stonebow Prim. Sch.
Stonebow Bridge
WESLEY CL.
ELIOT CL.
MELVILLE CL.
SEYMOUR CL.
BLACKBROOK ROAD
BUCKINGHAM DR.
LORRIMER WY.
AMIS CL.
HAILEY AV.
JAMES AV.
DUNCAN WY.
STEWART DR.
COOKSON PL.
EDEN CL.
DE MONTFORT CL.
BENNETT CL.
OSBORNE RD.
DOYLE CL.
HERRIOT WY.
Gorse Covert Centre
Comm. Cen.
FLEMING CL.
GALLICO CL.
CHARTERIS CL.
ORWELL CL.
Black Brook
WARWICK WAY
WAR. WICK WY.
WINDSOR
EPINAL WAY
Sir Robert Martin Ct.
Epinal Ct.
LEWIS
COPELAND CR.
Hanover Ct.
KINGSWOOD AV.
WHITBY CL.
LINDISFARNE DR.
GISBOROUGH WY.
BYLAND WY.
GRACE DR.
EASBY CL.
WAVERLEY CL.
MOUNT ST. OLAVES CL.
LILLESHALL WY.
RUFFORD CL.
Oxley Gutter
Dovecote
The Bungalow
SWITHLAND CL.
KENSINGTON AV.
SANDRINGHAM DR.
KINROSS CR.
HAWKER CL.
ACRE
HOWARD CL.
RAYNHAM DR.
CONWAY CL.
PETWORTH DR.
COTHELSTONE AV.
ASHDOWN CL.
CHATTH R.
STIRLING AV.
ROAD
TRELISSICK CL.
ALTHORPE DRIVE
COE AV.
KENILWORTH
LAMPORT CL.
WOBURN CL.
BLENHEIM CL.
WOLLATON AV.
OXBURGH CL.
HARDWICK DR.
THORPE HILL
Thorpe Ho.
KNIGHTTHORPE RD.
Knightthorpe Ct.
BURNS
TENNYSON
DUNHOLME AV.
LECKHAMPTON RD.
BROUGHTON CL.
CHISWICK CL.
OSTERLEY CL.
AVENUE
BROWNING RD.
LARKIN LA.
WORDSWORTH RD.
RUPERT BROOKE RD.
Garendon Park Obelisk
PRESTBURY RD.
MILDENHALL RD.
ROSEHILL
CLEEVE MNT.
OAKHURST CT.
ALAN MOSS
GARENDON
TRACKSIDE CL.
GARENDON PARK
Charnwood College (High)
Sports Centre
Playing Field
Charnwood College (Upper)
Ashmount School
Thorpe Acre Junior & Infant School
De Lisle Catholic School
Weir
STAPLEFORD PARK
Booth Wood
Booth Wood Prim. Sch.
Ten. Cts.
AFTON CL.
COWBRIDGE
CROSSWOOD CL.
GRACEDIEU WY.
BLACKBROOK
GARENDON ROAD
ASHBY CR.
COTSWOLD
Paula Athletics
High Performance Athletics
Sports Pitches
ECB Performance Cricket
Uni. Medical Cen.
LEIGHTON
BARDEN CL.
RAVENSTHORPE DR.
ROWBANK
ROUNDHILL WY.
HURSTWOOD
MIRES
BLITHFIELD AV.
CHELKER WY.
WILSTONE CL.
DRIVE
KNIPTON DR.
WINDLEDEN
Comm. Cen.
SCHOFIELD RD.
SHARPLEY RD.
ROAD
Shepherd's Hill
Temple of Venus
GRASSHOLME
HOWDEN CL.
DRIVE
LANESHAW AV.
EYEBROOK
DE LISLE CT.
OLD
HERMITAGE
NEW
MUMFORD
MARGARET
WAY
KEAY
Shortcliffe

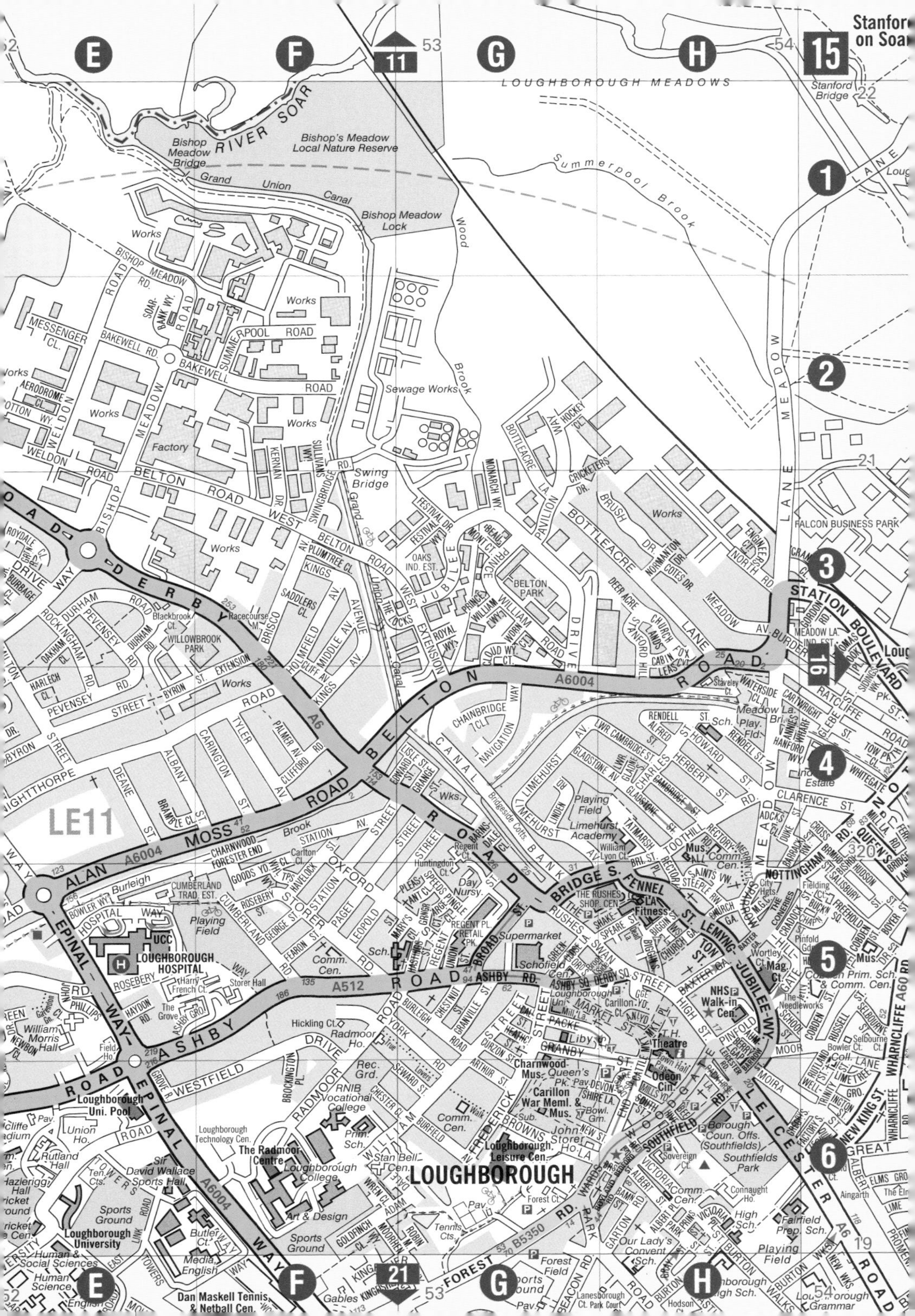

E
F
11
53
G
H
54
15
Stanford on Soar
LOUGHBOROUGH MEADOWS
Stanford Bridge
22
RIVER SOAR
Bishop Meadow Bridge
Bishop's Meadow Local Nature Reserve
Grand Union Canal
Bishop Meadow Lock
Summerpool Brook
Wood Brook
1
2
3
4
5
6
MEADOW LANE
Works
BISHOP MEADOW RD.
MESSENGER CL.
BAKEWELL RD.
SOAR-BANK WY.
SUMMERPOOL ROAD
BAKEWELL ROAD
AERODROME CL.
COTTON WY.
WELDON
WELDON ROAD
Factory
Sewage Works
KERNAN DR.
SULLIVANS WY.
SWINGBRIDGE RD.
Swing Bridge
BELTON ROAD WEST
BELTON ROAD WEST EXTENSION
HOCKEY CL.
BOTTLEACRE WAY
CRICKETERS DR.
PAVILION LA.
MONARCH WY.
FESTIVAL DR.
OAKS IND. EST.
JUBILEE
BELTON PARK
BRUSH DR.
BOTTLEACRE
NORMANTON DR.
COTES DR.
ENGINEER CT.
NORTH RD.
FALCON BUSINESS PARK
21
STATION BOULEVARD
MEADOW LA. IND. EST.
16
BURDER ROAD
A6004
BELTON ROAD
DERBY ROAD
A6
ALAN MOSS ROAD
PEVENSEY RD.
DURHAM ROAD
WILLOWBROOK PARK
Racecourse
BYRON ST.
Works
TYLER AV.
CARINGTON ST.
PALMER AV.
CLIFFORD RD.
CHAINBRIDGE CL.
NAVIGATION WAY
CANAL BANK
RENDELL ST.
HOWARD ST.
HERBERT ST.
CHARLES ST.
GLADSTONE AV.
LIMEHURST AV.
Playing Field
Limehurst Academy
RATCLIFFE RD.
CLARENCE ST.
NOTTINGHAM RD.
QUEEN'S RD.
LE11
CHARNWOOD FORESTER END
STATION ST.
OXFORD ST.
CUMBERLAND TRAD. EST.
Playing Field
HOSPITAL WAY
UCC
LOUGHBOROUGH HOSPITAL
EPINAL WAY
ASHBY ROAD
A512
Day Nursy.
REGENT PL. RETAIL PK.
Supermarket
BRIDGE ST.
FENNEL ST.
LEMYNGTON ST.
THE RUSHES SHOP. CEN.
LA Fitness
Mus.
NHS Walk-in Cen.
JUBILEE WAY
Theatre
Town Hall
Odeon Cin.
Charnwood Mus.
Queen's Pk.
Carillon War Meml. & Mus.
MARKET PL.
GRANBY ST.
Liby.
Loughborough Uni.
Hickling Ct.
Radmoor Ho.
RADMOOR RD.
Rec. Grd.
RNIB Vocational College
Comm. Cen.
Loughborough Leisure Cen.
John Storer Ho.
LOUGHBOROUGH
Loughborough Uni. Pool
Loughborough Technology Cen.
The Radmoor Centre
Loughborough College
Art & Design
Sir David Wallace Sports Hall
Sports Ground
Loughborough University
Butler Ct.
Media, English
Human & Social Sciences
Human Science
Dan Maskell Tennis & Netball Cen.
A6004
FOREST RD.
B5350
Forest Field
Tennis Cts.
Pav.
Borough Coun. Offs. (Southfields)
Southfields Park
SOUTHFIELD RD.
WOODGATE
LEICESTER ROAD
A6
Fairfield Prep. Sch.
Playing Field
High Sch.
Our Lady's Convent Sch.
Comm. Cen.
BURTON WALKS
Loughborough Grammar
Loughborough High Sch.
Hodson
Lanesborough Ct. Park Court
Gables
21
WHARNCLIFFE
GREAT CENTRAL
Selbourne Coll.
The Needleworks
Cobden Prim. Sch. & Comm. Cen.
MOIRA ST.
19
320

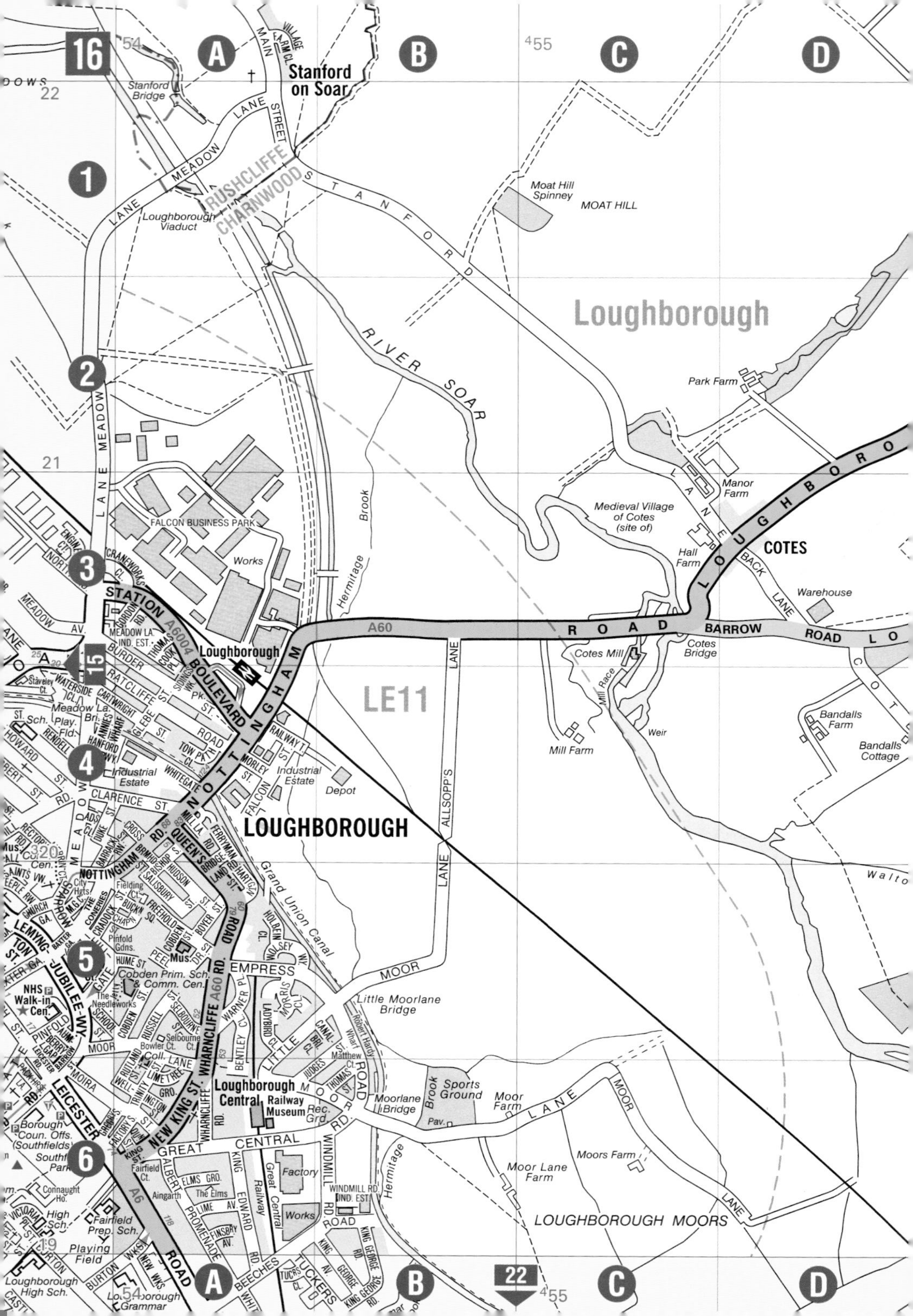
Stanford on Soar
Stanford Bridge
Loughborough Viaduct
RUSHCLIFFE
CHARNWOOD
Moat Hill Spinney
MOAT HILL
Loughborough
RIVER SOAR
Park Farm
Manor Farm
Medieval Village of Cotes (site of)
Hall Farm
COTES
Warehouse
FALCON BUSINESS PARK
Works
LOUGHBOROUGH ROAD
BARROW ROAD
A60
Cotes Mill
Cotes Bridge
Mill Race
Weir
Mill Farm
Bandalls Farm
Bandalls Cottage
LE11
ALLSOPP'S LANE
Industrial Estate
Depot
LOUGHBOROUGH
NOTTINGHAM ROAD
STATION BOULEVARD
A6004
Grand Union Canal
Hermitage Brook
MOOR LANE
Little Moorlane Bridge
Moorlane Bridge
Sports Ground
Moor Farm
Moors Farm
Moor Lane Farm
LOUGHBOROUGH MOORS
Loughborough Central Railway Museum
Rec. Grd.
GREAT CENTRAL RD.
Factory
Works
WINDMILL RD. IND. EST.
NHS Walk-in Cen.
Cobden Prim. Sch. & Comm. Cen.
Pinfold Gdns.
Mus.
Borough Coun. Offs. (Southfields)
Southfield Park
Fairfield Prep. Sch.
Playing Field
Loughborough High Sch.
Loughborough Grammar
LEICESTER RD.
NEW KING ST.
WHARNCLIFFE RD.
A6
Walton
455
54
22
21
20
19

15
22

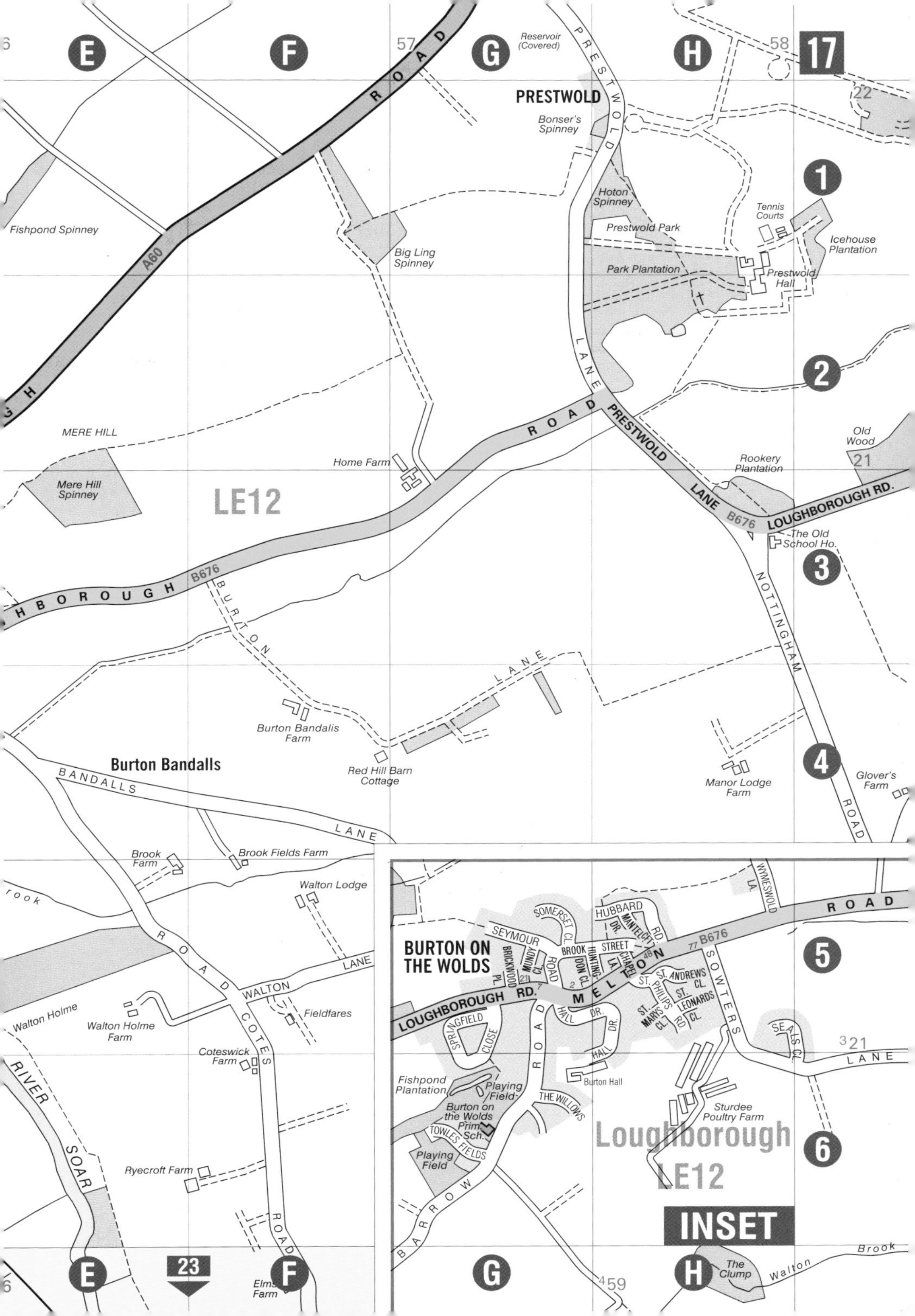

E F 57 G 58

PRESTWOLD

Reservoir (Covered)

Bonser's Spinney

H

22

Fishpond Spinney

Hoton Spinney

Tennis Courts

1

Prestwold Park

Icehouse Plantation

Big Ling Spinney

Park Plantation

Prestwold Hall

A60

2

ROAD

MERE HILL

ROAD PRESTWOLD

Old Wood

21

Mere Hill Spinney

Home Farm

LANE

Rookery Plantation

LE12

LANE B676 LOUGHBOROUGH RD.

The Old School Ho.

HBOROUGH B676

BURTON

3

NOTTINGHAM

LANE

Burton Bandalls

Burton Bandalls Farm

Red Hill Barn Cottage

Manor Lodge Farm

4

ROAD

Glover's Farm

BANDALLS

LANE

Brook Farm

Brook Fields Farm

Walton Lodge

rook

WYMESWOLD LA.

ROAD

BURTON ON THE WOLDS

HUBBARD

SOMERSET CL.

MANTLE RD.

ROAD

R O A D

5

SEYMOUR

BROOK ST

STREET

77 B676

BRICKWOOD PL.

UNIUM CL

HINTON CL

CHAPEL

ST. ANDREWS CL.

SOWTERS

LOUGHBOROUGH RD.

M E L T O N

ST. PHILIPS CL.

ST. LEONARDS CL.

Walton Holme

Walton Holme Farm

WALTON

ROAD

LANE

COTES

Fieldfares

SPRINGFIELD CLOSE

ST. MARYS CL.

SEALS CL.

LANE

3 21

Coteswick Farm

HALL DR.

HALL DR.

RIVER

SOAR

Fishpond Plantation

Playing Field

Burton on the Wolds Prim. Sch.

THE WILLOWS

Burton Hall

Sturdee Poultry Farm

Loughborough

6

Ryecroft Farm

TOWLES FIELDS

Playing Field

LE12

BARROW

ROAD

INSET

E **23** F G 459 H

The Clump

Elms Farm

Brook Walton

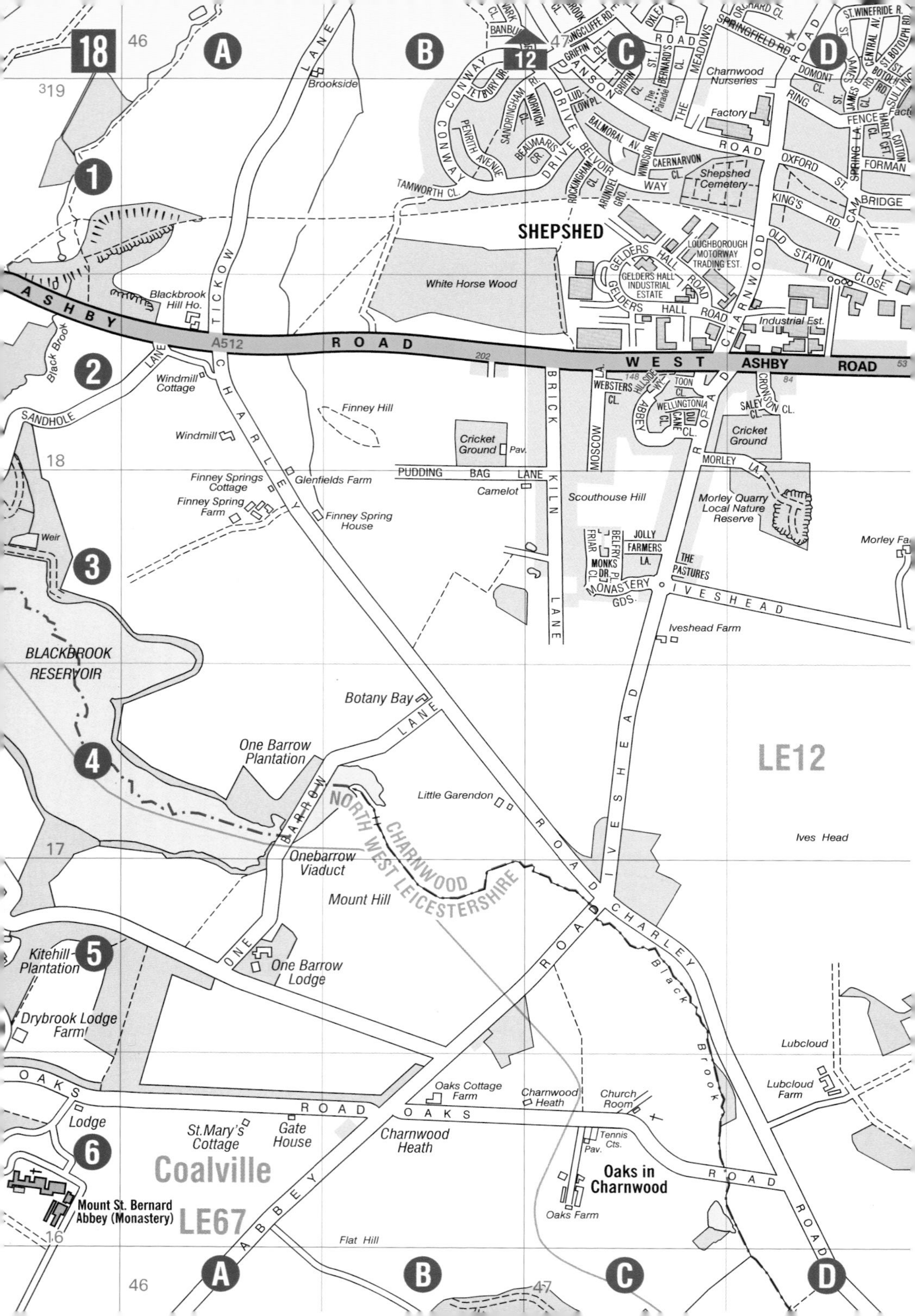

18
12
A
B
C
D
1
2
3
4
5
6
46
47
319
18
17
16
SHEPSHED
Brookside
Charnwood Nurseries
Factory
Shepshed Cemetery
LOUGHBOROUGH MOTORWAY TRADING EST.
GELDERS HALL INDUSTRIAL ESTATE
Industrial Est.
White Horse Wood
Blackbrook Hill Ho.
ASHBY ROAD
A512
WEST ASHBY ROAD
Black Brook
Windmill Cottage
Windmill
SANDHOLE
Finney Hill
Cricket Ground
Pav.
PUDDING BAG LANE
Camelot
Glenfields Farm
Finney Springs Cottage
Finney Spring Farm
Finney Spring House
Scouthouse Hill
Morley Quarry Local Nature Reserve
Morley Fa
Weir
BLACKBROOK RESERVOIR
Iveshead Farm
IVESHEAD
Botany Bay
LE12
One Barrow Plantation
Little Garendon
Ives Head
NORTH WEST LEICESTERSHIRE
CHARNWOOD
Onebarrow Viaduct
Mount Hill
Kitehill Plantation
One Barrow Lodge
Drybrook Lodge Farm
Lubcloud
Lubcloud Farm
Oaks Cottage Farm
Charnwood Heath
Church Room
OAKS ROAD
Lodge
St.Mary's Cottage
Gate House
Tennis Cts.
Oaks in Charnwood
Oaks Farm
Coalville
LE67
Mount St. Bernard Abbey (Monastery)
Flat Hill
ABBEY ROAD
CHARLEY ROAD
TICKOW LANE
ONE BARROW LANE
BRICK KILN LANE
CHARNWOOD ROAD
MORLEY LA.
OXFORD ST.
KING'S RD.
OLD STATION CLOSE
CAMBRIDGE
RING FENCE
FORMAN
CAERNARVON CL.
BELVOIR WAY
BALMORAL AV.
WINDSOR DR.
CONWAY
PENRITH AVENUE
TAMWORTH CL.
SANDRINGHAM RI.
BEAUMARIS CR.
DANSON
GRIFFIN CL.
THE MEADOWS
SPRINGFIELD RD.
DOMONT CL.
ROCKINGHAM CL.
ARUNDEL GRO.
MOSCOW LA.
WEBSTERS CL.
ABBEY
TOON CL.
WELLINGTONIA CL.
CRONSON CL.
SALEY CL.
JOLLY FARMERS LA.
THE PASTURES
MONASTERY GDS.
MONKS DR.
FRIAR CL.
BELFRY PL.
Black Brook

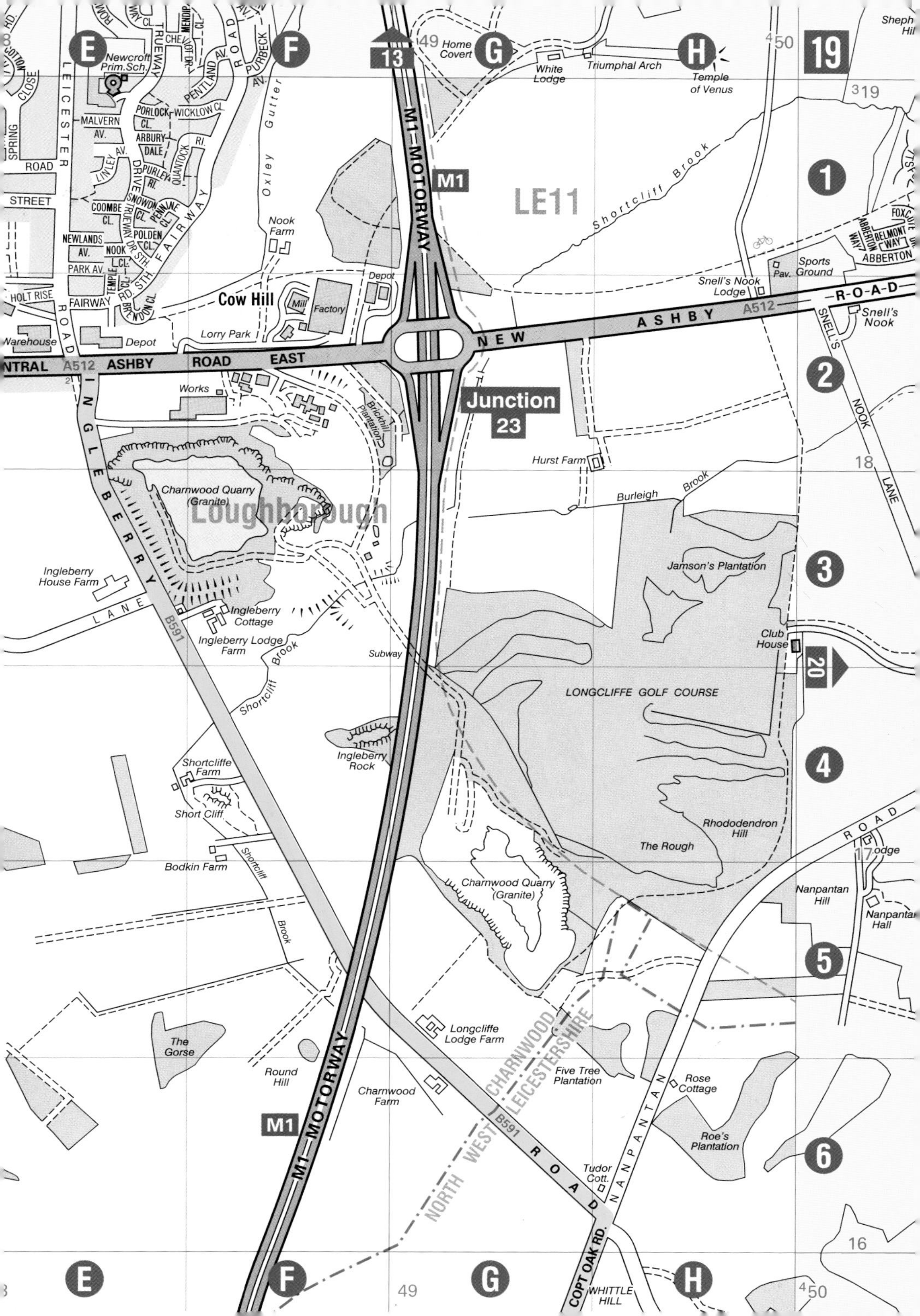

19
13
20
E
F
G
H
Newcroft Prim.Sch.
Home Covert
White Lodge
Triumphal Arch
Temple of Venus
LE11
M1
M1 MOTORWAY
Shortcliff Brook
Oxley Gutter
Nook Farm
Cow Hill
Mill
Factory
Depot
Lorry Park
Warehouse
Sports Ground
Pav.
Snell's Nook Lodge
Snell's Nook
NEW ASHBY ROAD
A512
ASHBY ROAD EAST
CENTRAL
Junction 23
Works
Brickhill Plantation
Hurst Farm
Burleigh Brook
Charnwood Quarry (Granite)
Loughborough
Jamson's Plantation
Ingleberry House Farm
INGLEBERRY LANE
B591
Ingleberry Cottage
Ingleberry Lodge Farm
Subway
Club House
LONGCLIFFE GOLF COURSE
Ingleberry Rock
Shortcliffe Farm
Short Cliff
Bodkin Farm
Rhododendron Hill
The Rough
Lodge
Nanpantan Hill
Nanpantan Hall
The Gorse
Round Hill
Longcliffe Lodge Farm
Charnwood Farm
CHARNWOOD LEICESTERSHIRE
NORTH WEST
Five Tree Plantation
Rose Cottage
Roe's Plantation
Tudor Cott.
NANPANTAN ROAD
B591 ROAD
COPT OAK RD.
WHITTLE HILL
SNELL'S NOOK LANE
ABBERTON
BELMONT WAY
FOXCOTE
FAIRWAY
TRUEWAY
PENTLAND AV.
PURBECK AV.
PORLOCK
WICKLOW CL.
MALVERN AV.
ARBURY
DALE
PURLEY RI.
QUANTOCK RI.
COOMBE CL.
SNOWDON CL.
PENNINE CL.
POLDEN CL.
NEWLANDS AV.
NOOK CL.
PARK AV.
TEMPLE CL.
BRENDON CL.
HOLT RISE
LEICESTER ROAD
SPRING CLOSE
STREET
CHEVIOT DR.
MENDIP CL.
450
49
1
2
3
4
5
6
319
18
17
16

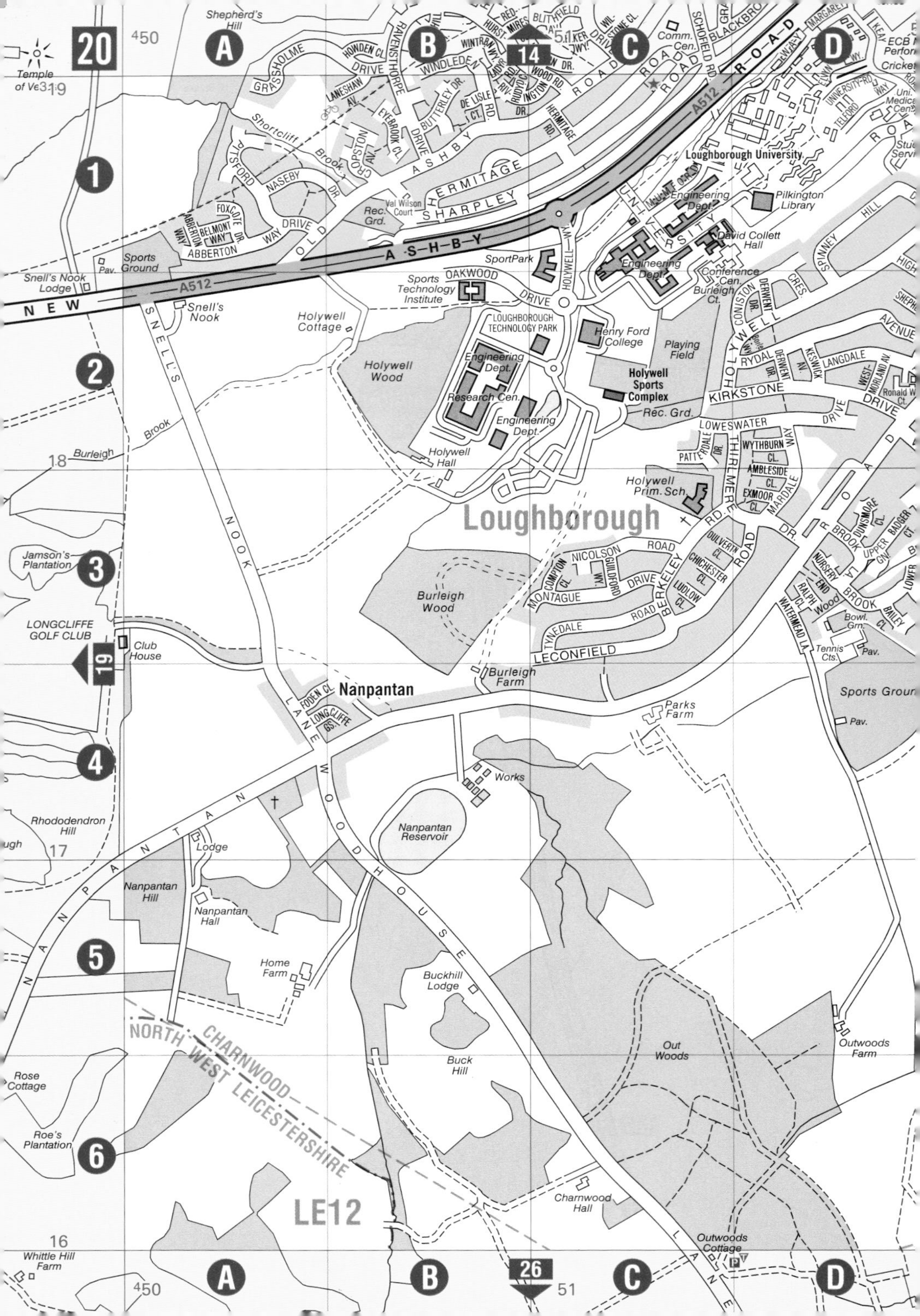
20
450
A
B
C
D
14
26
51
1
2
3
4
5
6
19
18
17
16
Temple of Venus
Shepherd's Hill
Grassholme Drive
Howden Cl.
Ravensthorpe
Windleden
Wintrin Wy.
Red Hurst
Mires
Blithfield
Comm. Cen.
Schofield Rd.
Blackbrook
Margaret
Keay
ECB Performance
Cricket
Laneshaw Av.
Eyebrook Cl.
Butterley Dr.
De Lisle Ct.
Hermitage Rd.
Ashby Road
Shortcliff Brook
Pitsford
Naseby Dr.
Cropston Av.
Foxcote Dr.
Belmont Way
Abberton Way
Abberton
Old Ashby Road
Drive
Rec. Grd.
Val Wilson Court
Hermitage
Sharpley
A512
New Ashby Road
Sports Ground
Pav.
Snell's Nook Lodge
Snell's Nook
Snells Nook Lane
Loughborough University
Engineering Dept.
Pilkington Library
University Rd
Telford Way
Uni. Medical Cen.
Student Services
David Collett Hall
Conference Cen.
Burleigh Ct.
SportPark
Holywell Way
Oakwood Drive
Sports Technology Institute
Holywell Cottage
Holywell Wood
Loughborough Technology Park
Research Cen.
Henry Ford College
Playing Field
Holywell Sports Complex
Rec. Grd.
Holywell Hall
Holywell Drive
Coniston Dr.
Derwent
Spinney Hill
Rydal
Keswick Av.
Langdale
Westmorland Av
Avenue
Kirkstone
Loweswater
Thirlmere Rd.
Patterdale Dr.
Wythburn Cl.
Ambleside Cl.
Exmoor Cl.
Mardale Way
Holywell Prim. Sch.
Loughborough
Brook
Burleigh
Jamson's Plantation
Longcliffe Golf Club
Club House
Burleigh Wood
Nicolson Road
Compton Cl.
Guildford Wy.
Montague Drive
Dulverton Cl.
Chichester Cl.
Ludlow Cl.
Berkeley Road
Tynedale Road
Leconfield
Burleigh Farm
Nanpantan
Foden Cl.
Longcliffe Gs.
Parks Farm
Brook Lane
Nursery End
Ralph Cl.
Watermead La.
Wood Brook
Bailey Cl.
Upper Gn.
Badger Ct.
Dunsmore Cl.
Bowl. Grn.
Tennis Cts.
Sports Ground
Works
Nanpantan Reservoir
Rhododendron Hill
Lodge
Nanpantan Hill
Nanpantan Hall
Nanpantan Road
Woodhouse Lane
Home Farm
Buckhill Lodge
Buck Hill
Out Woods
Outwoods Farm
Charnwood
North West Leicestershire
Rose Cottage
Roe's Plantation
LE12
Charnwood Hall
Outwoods Cottage
Whittle Hill Farm

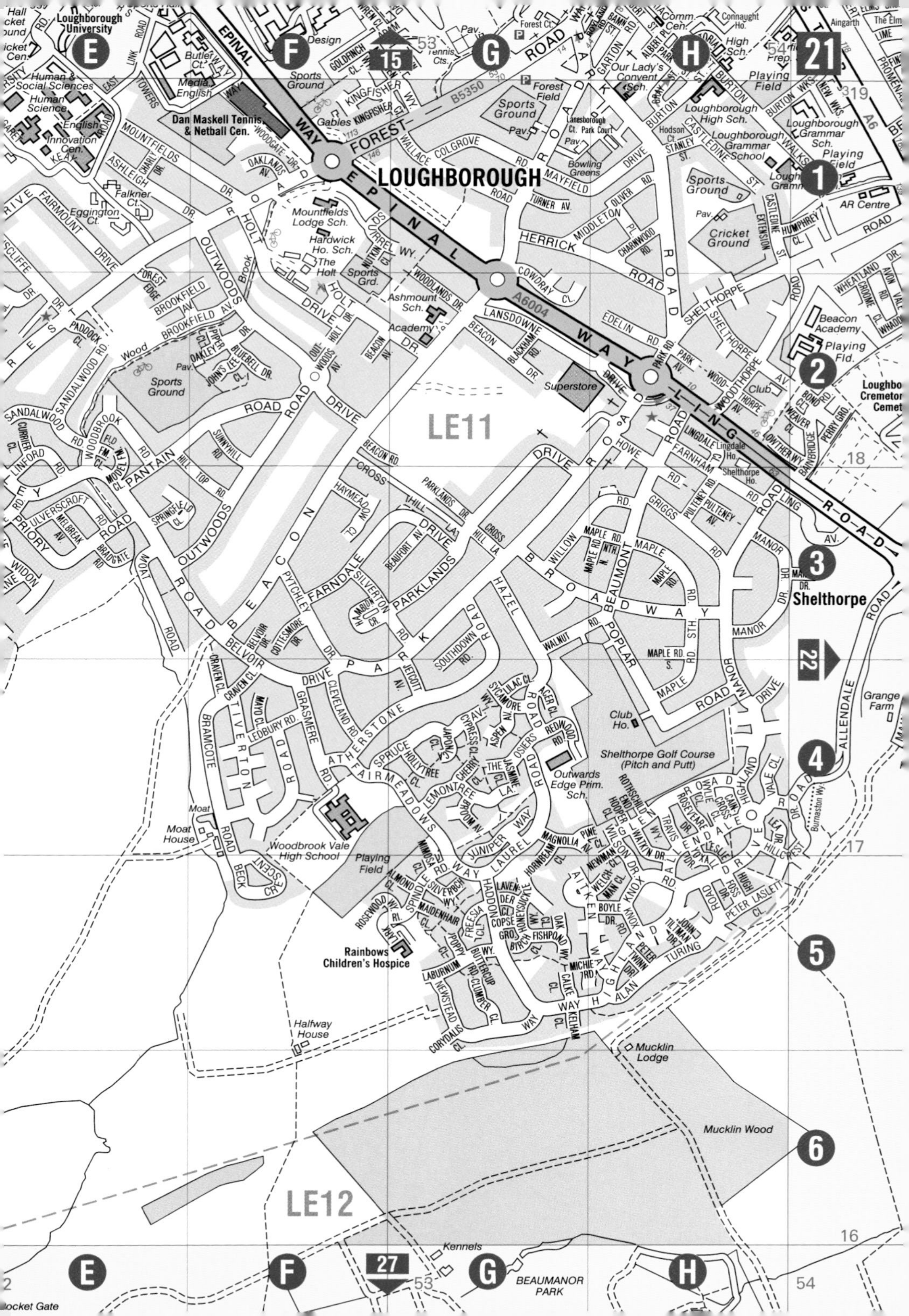
LOUGHBOROUGH
LE11
LE12
Shelthorpe
Loughborough University
Human & Social Sciences
Human Science
English
Innovation Cen.
Butler Ct.
Media, English
Design
Dan Maskell Tennis & Netball Cen.
Sports Ground
Gables
Tennis Cts.
Forest Ct.
Forest Field
Comm. Cen.
Connaught Ho.
High Sch.
Our Lady's Convent Sch.
Playing Field
Loughborough High Sch.
Loughborough Grammar Sch.
Loughborough Grammar School
Hodson Ct.
Lanesborough Ct.
Park Court
Bowling Greens
Cricket Ground
AR Centre
Beacon Academy
Playing Fld.
Loughborough Crematorium
Club
Lingdale Ho.
Shelthorpe Ho.
Mountfields Lodge Sch.
Hardwick Ho. Sch.
The Holt
Sports Grd.
Ashmount Sch.
Academy
Superstore
Wood
Sports Ground
Falkner Ct.
Eggington Ct.
EPINAL WAY
FOREST ROAD
B5350
A6004
A6
HOLT DRIVE
HERRICK ROAD
BEACON ROAD
BEACON DRIVE
PARK ROAD
OUTWOODS ROAD
OUTWOODS DRIVE
PANTAIN ROAD
WOODBROOK ROAD
BROADWAY
BEAUMONT ROAD
MAPLE ROAD
MANOR ROAD
MANOR DRIVE
ATHERSTONE ROAD
PARK DRIVE
ASHBY ROAD
BELVOIR DRIVE
FAIRMEADOWS WAY
LAUREL WAY
HIGHLAND DRIVE
ALLENDALE ROAD
ALLENDALE
MOAT ROAD
Moat
Moat House
Woodbrook Vale High School
Playing Field
Club Ho.
Shelthorpe Golf Course (Pitch and Putt)
Outwards Edge Prim. Sch.
Rainbows Children's Hospice
Halfway House
Mucklin Lodge
Mucklin Wood
Grange Farm
Kennels
BEAUMANOR PARK
Hocket Gate
E
F
G
H
1
2
3
4
5
6
15
22
27
53
54
16
17
18
19

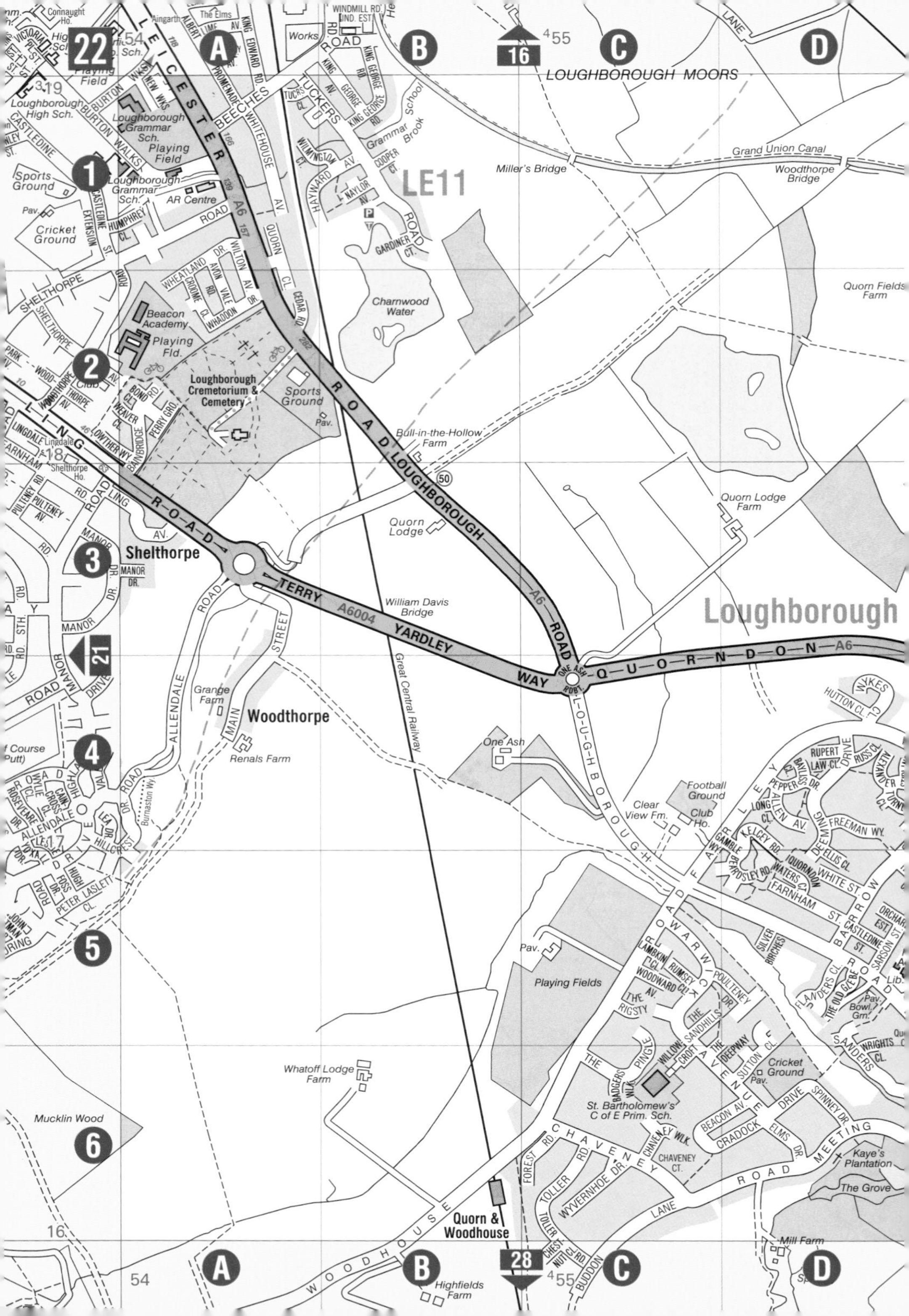

22
A
B
C
D
16
LOUGHBOROUGH MOORS
LE11
Loughborough High Sch.
Loughborough Grammar Sch.
Playing Field
AR Centre
Sports Ground
Cricket Ground
Beacon Academy
Playing Fld.
Loughborough Crematorium & Cemetery
Sports Ground
Charnwood Water
Miller's Bridge
Grand Union Canal
Woodthorpe Bridge
Quorn Fields Farm
Bull-in-the-Hollow Farm
Quorn Lodge
Quorn Lodge Farm
Shelthorpe
William Davis Bridge
Loughborough
LEICESTER ROAD
LOUGHBOROUGH ROAD
TERRY YARDLEY WAY
QUORNDON
ONE ASH RDBT.
Grange Farm
Woodthorpe
Renals Farm
Great Central Railway
One Ash
Football Ground
Clear View Fm.
Club Ho.
Playing Fields
Cricket Ground
St. Bartholomew's C of E Prim. Sch.
Whatoff Lodge Farm
Mucklin Wood
Kaye's Plantation
The Grove
Mill Farm
Quorn & Woodhouse
Highfields Farm
WOODHOUSE
CHAVENEY
MEETING
BUDDON
21
28
1
2
3
4
5
6

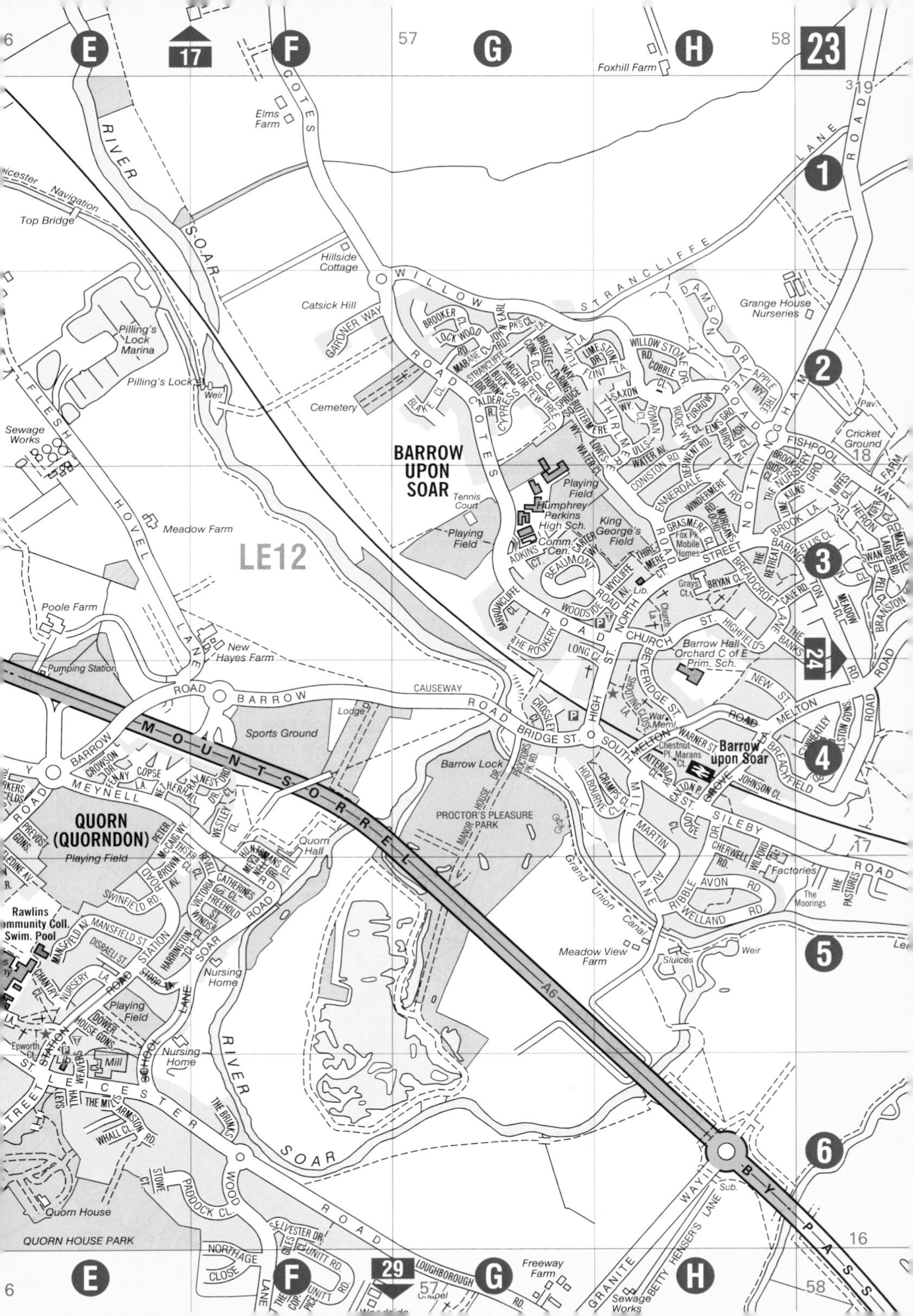
BARROW UPON SOAR
QUORN (QUORNDON)
LE12
River Soar
Leicester Navigation
Top Bridge
Pilling's Lock Marina
Pilling's Lock
Weir
Sewage Works
Meadow Farm
Poole Farm
Pumping Station
New Hayes Farm
Elms Farm
Foxhill Farm
Hillside Cottage
Catsick Hill
Cemetery
Tennis Court
Playing Field
Humphrey Perkins High Sch.
King George's Field
Comm. Cen.
Fox Pk Mobile Homes
Grange House Nurseries
Cricket Ground
Pav.
Barrow Hall Orchard C of E Prim. Sch.
War Meml
Barrow upon Soar
Sports Ground
Lodge
Barrow Lock
PROCTOR'S PLEASURE PARK
Quorn Hall
Grand Union Canal
Meadow View Farm
Sluices
Factories
The Moorings
Nursing Home
Rawlins Community Coll. Swim. Pool
Quorn House
QUORN HOUSE PARK
Freeway Farm
Sewage Works
Epworth Ct.
Mill
Lib.
MOUNTSORREL BY PASS
A6
BARROW ROAD
CAUSEWAY
BRIDGE ST.
HIGH ST.
SOUTH ST.
NORTH ST.
CHURCH ST.
MELTON ROAD
SILEBY ROAD
NOTTINGHAM ROAD
STRANCLIFFE LANE
WILLOW ROAD
COTES ROAD
FISHPOOL WAY
HOVEL LANE
FLESH HOVEL LANE
MEYNELL ROAD
LEICESTER ROAD
STATION ROAD
SCHOOL LANE
WOOD LANE
LOUGHBOROUGH RD.
GRANITE WAY
BETTY HENSER'S LANE
MILL LANE
GROVE LA.
BREACHFIELD RD.
JOHNSON CL.
17
29
24
E F G H
1 2 3 4 5 6
57 58 16 17 18 19

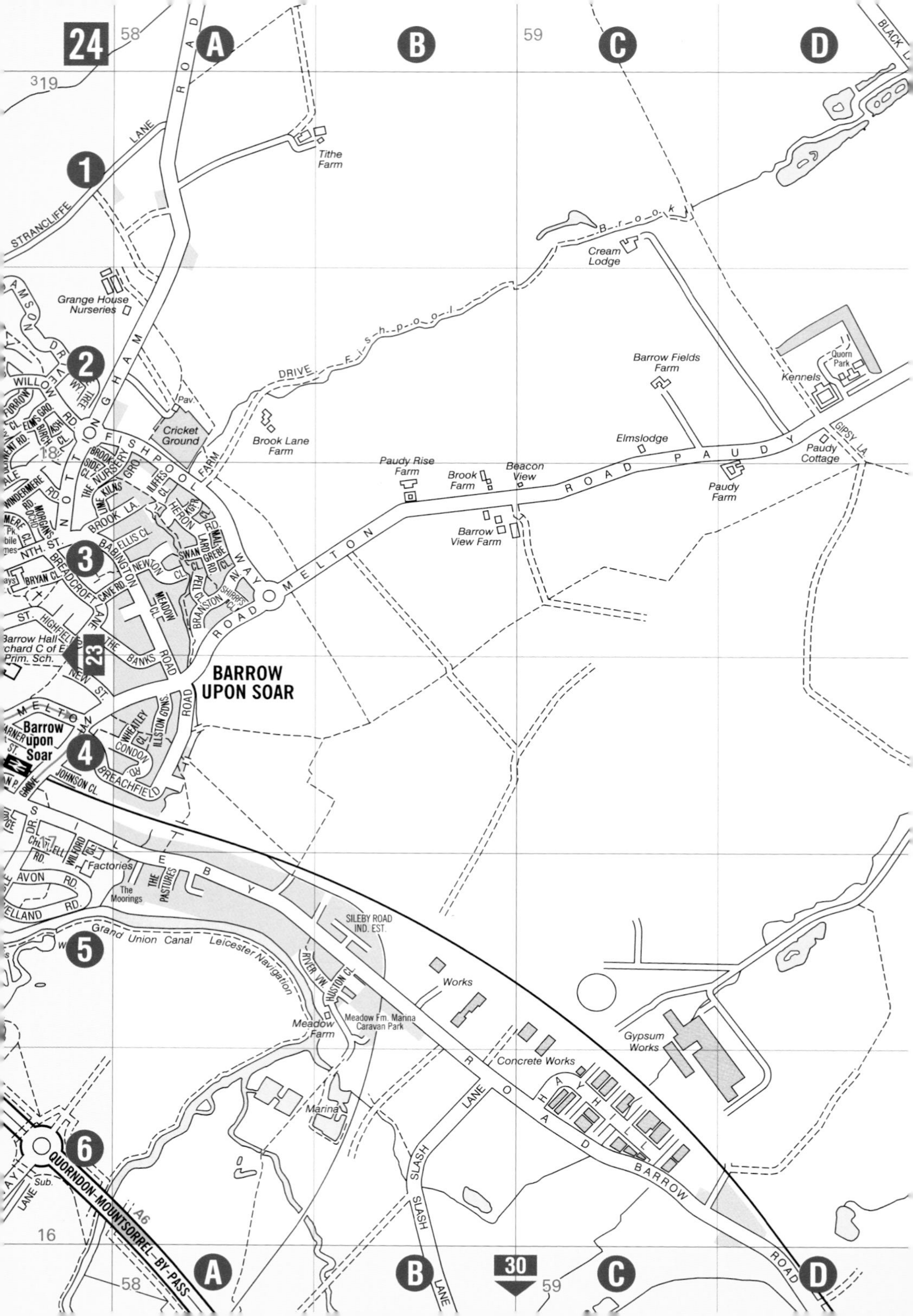

A **B** **C** **D**

1

STRANCLIFFE

Tithe
Farm

B r o o k

Cream
Lodge

LANE

ROAD

Grange House
Nurseries

2

WILLOW

FIBROW

TREE

NOTTINGHAM

FISHPOOL

FARM

DRIVE

F i s h p o o l

Barrow Fields
Farm

Quorn
Park

Kennels

Pav.

Cricket
Ground

Brook Lane
Farm

Elmslodge

GIPSY LA.

Paudy
Cottage

18

THE NURSERY

Paudy Rise
Farm

Brook
Farm

Beacon
View

ROAD   PAUDY

Paudy
Farm

3

WINDERMERE RD

MERE
RD.

NTH. ST.

BRYAN CL.

BREADCROFT

BROOK LA.

KING'S
RD.

ELLIS CL.

BABINGTON

CAVE RD.

NEW CL.

SWAN
CL.

HERON

LARD GRERE

MEADOW
CL.

BRANSTON

TTH.

CL.

MELTON

WAY

ROAD

Barrow Hall
chard C of E
Prim. Sch.

23

HIGHFIELD

ST.

CAVE LANE

BANKS

NEW ST.

ROAD

Beacon
View

Barrow
View Farm

**BARROW
UPON SOAR**

MELTON

Barrow
upon
Soar

WHEATLEY

WEATLEY

CONDON

ALLISTON DOWNS

BREACHFIELD

RD

4

JOHNSON CL.

Ch.

RD.

MILFORD

AVON

RD.

WELLAND   RD.

Factories

The
Pastures

THE   PASTURES

B

SILEBY ROAD
IND. EST.

The
Moorings

RIVER VW.

AUSTIN CL.

Y

5

Grand Union Canal   Leicester Navigation

Works

Meadow
Farm

Meadow Fm. Marina
Caravan Park

SLASH

LANE

Concrete Works

HAYBL

Gypsum
Works

ROAD

Marina

BARROW

6

Sub.

QUORNDON - MOUNTSORREL - BY-PASS

A6

LANE

16

SLASH

LANE

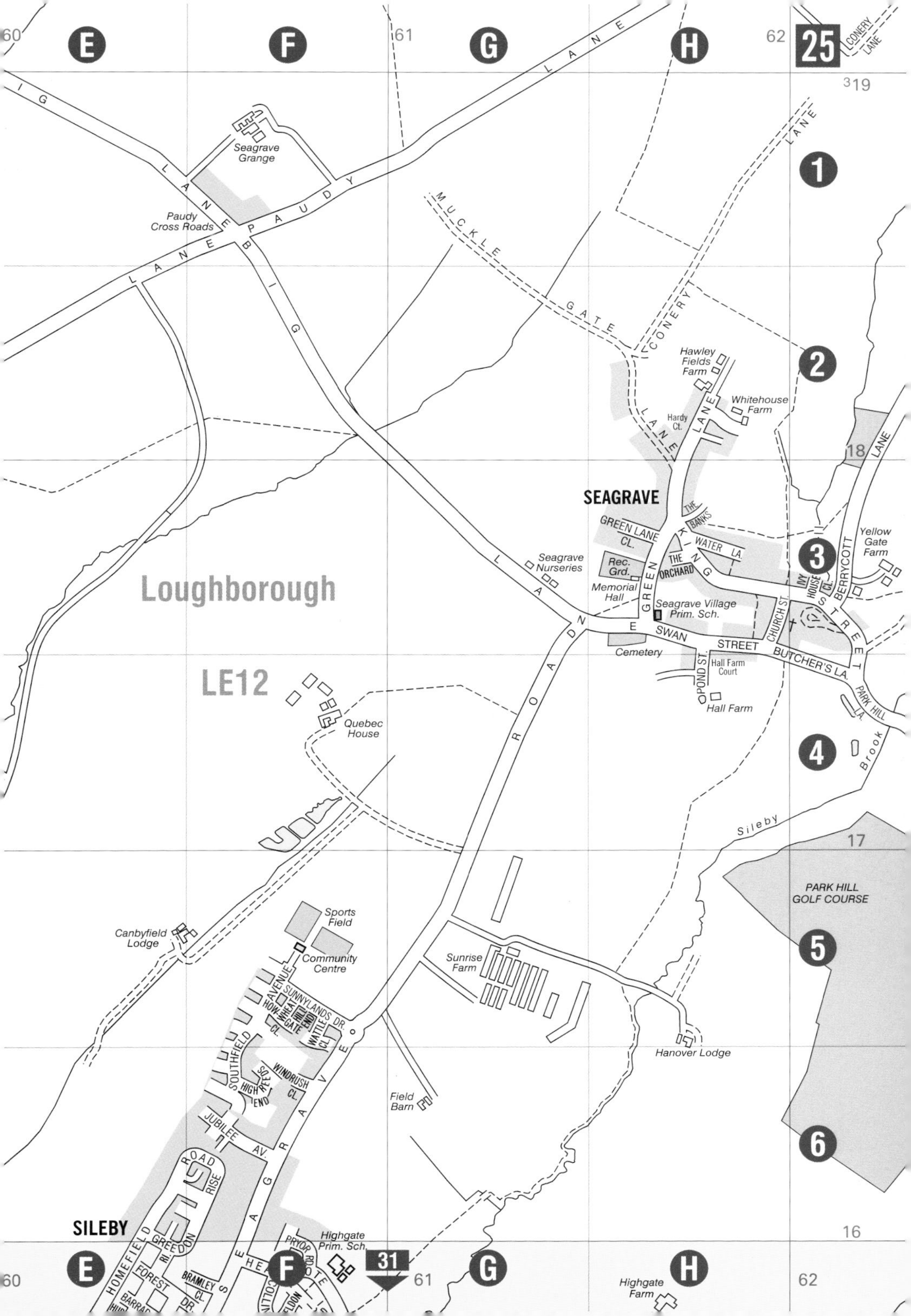

E
F
G
H
60
61
62
319
1
2
3
4
5
6
18
17
16
CONERY LANE
IG LANE
PAUDY LANE
Seagrave Grange
Paudy Cross Roads
MUCKLE GATE
CONERY LANE
Hawley Fields Farm
Whitehouse Farm
Hardy Ct.
SEAGRAVE
THE BANKS
GREEN LANE CL.
WATER LA.
THE ORCHARD
KING STREET
Yellow Gate Farm
BERRYCOTT LANE
IVY HOUSE CL.
Seagrave Nurseries
Rec. Grd.
Memorial Hall
GREEN
Seagrave Village Prim. Sch.
SWAN STREET
CHURCH ST.
BUTCHER'S LA.
PARK HILL LA.
Cemetery
POND ST.
Hall Farm Court
Hall Farm
Loughborough
LE12
Quebec House
Brook
Sileby
PARK HILL GOLF COURSE
Sports Field
Canbyfield Lodge
Community Centre
AVENUE
SUNNYLANDS DR.
WHEAT HILL END
HOW GATE CL.
WATTLE CL.
Sunrise Farm
SOUTHFIELD
WINDRUSH CL.
HIGH END
REES
Field Barn
Hanover Lodge
JUBILEE AV.
SEAGRAVE ROAD
ROAD RISE
SILEBY
HOMEFIELD
GREEDON RI.
FOREST DR.
BRAMLEY CL.
Highgate Prim. Sch.
PRYOR ROAD
31
Highgate Farm

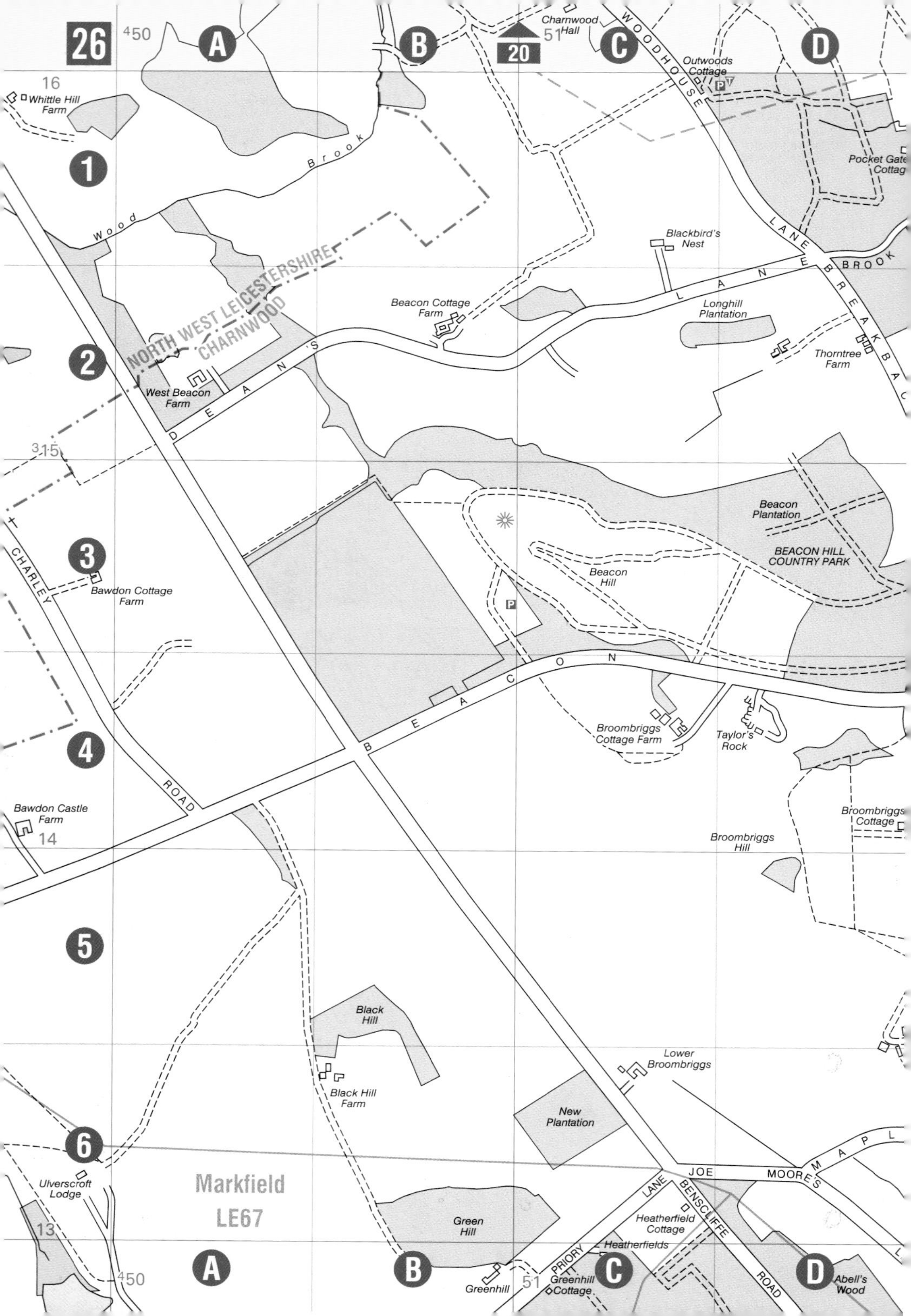

26 450

16

1

2

3

4

5

6

A   B   C   D

Whittle Hill Farm

Charnwood Hall

51

20

Outwoods Cottage

Pocket Gate Cottage

WOODHOUSE

LANE BREAKBACK BROOK

Brook

Wood

NORTH WEST LEICESTERSHIRE
CHARNWOOD

Blackbird's Nest

Beacon Cottage Farm

Longhill Plantation

Thorntree Farm

West Beacon Farm

315

Beacon Plantation

BEACON HILL COUNTRY PARK

CHARLEY

Bawdon Cottage Farm

Beacon Hill

P

Broombriggs Cottage Farm

Taylor's Rock

ROAD

Broombriggs Cottage

Bawdon Castle Farm

14

BEACON

Broombriggs Hill

Black Hill

Lower Broombriggs

New Plantation

Black Hill Farm

Markfield
LE67

Ulverscroft Lodge

13

JOE MOORES

MAPL

Green Hill

Heatherfield Cottage

PRIORY LANE

BENSCLIFFE

Heatherfields

450

A   B   C   D

Greenhill

51

Greenhill Cottage

ROAD

Abell's Wood

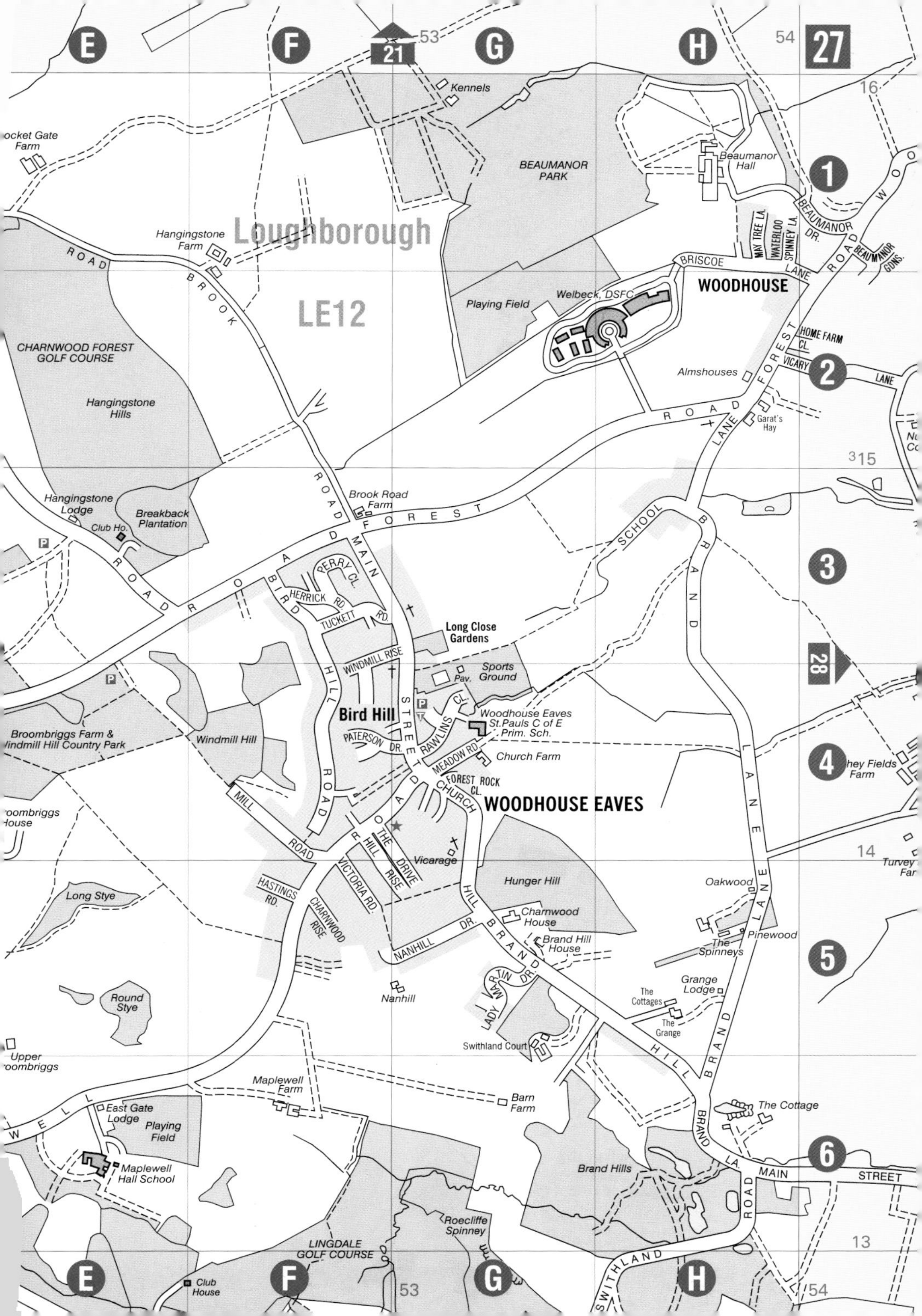

E
F
G
H
21
53
54
16
15
14
13
1
2
3
4
5
6
28
Loughborough
LE12
Kennels
ocket Gate Farm
BEAUMANOR PARK
Beaumanor Hall
BEAUMANOR DR.
MAY TREE LA.
WATERLOO
SPINNEY LA.
BRISCOE LANE
BEAUMANOR GDNS.
WOODHOUSE
Hangingstone Farm
ROAD BROOK
Playing Field
Welbeck, DSFC
HOME FARM CL.
VICARY LANE
Almshouses
CHARNWOOD FOREST GOLF COURSE
Hangingstone Hills
ROAD FOREST LANE
Garat's Hay
Hangingstone Lodge
Breakback Plantation
Club Ho.
Brook Road Farm
FOREST ROAD
MAIN
SCHOOL
BRAND LANE
PERRY CL.
BIRD
HERRICK RD.
TUCKETT RD.
Long Close Gardens
WINDMILL RISE
HILL
Sports Ground
Pav.
Bird Hill
STREET
RAWLINS CL.
Woodhouse Eaves St.Pauls C of E Prim. Sch.
Broombriggs Farm & Windmill Hill Country Park
Windmill Hill
PATERSON DR.
MEADOW RD.
Church Farm
hey Fields Farm
FOREST ROCK CL.
CHURCH
WOODHOUSE EAVES
roombriggs House
MILL ROAD
ROAD
THE DRIVE
HILL RISE
Vicarage
Turvey Far
HASTINGS RD.
VICTORIA RD.
CHARNWOOD RISE
Hunger Hill
Oakwood
Long Stye
Charnwood House
NANHILL DR.
Brand Hill House
BRAND
The Spinneys
Pinewood
Round Stye
Nanhill
LADY MARTIN DR.
The Cottages
Grange Lodge
The Grange
Swithland Court
Upper roombriggs
Maplewell Farm
Barn Farm
The Cottage
WELL
East Gate Lodge
Playing Field
Maplewell Hall School
Brand Hills
BRAND LA.
MAIN STREET
ROAD
Roecliffe Spinney
LINGDALE GOLF COURSE
Club House
SWITHLAND

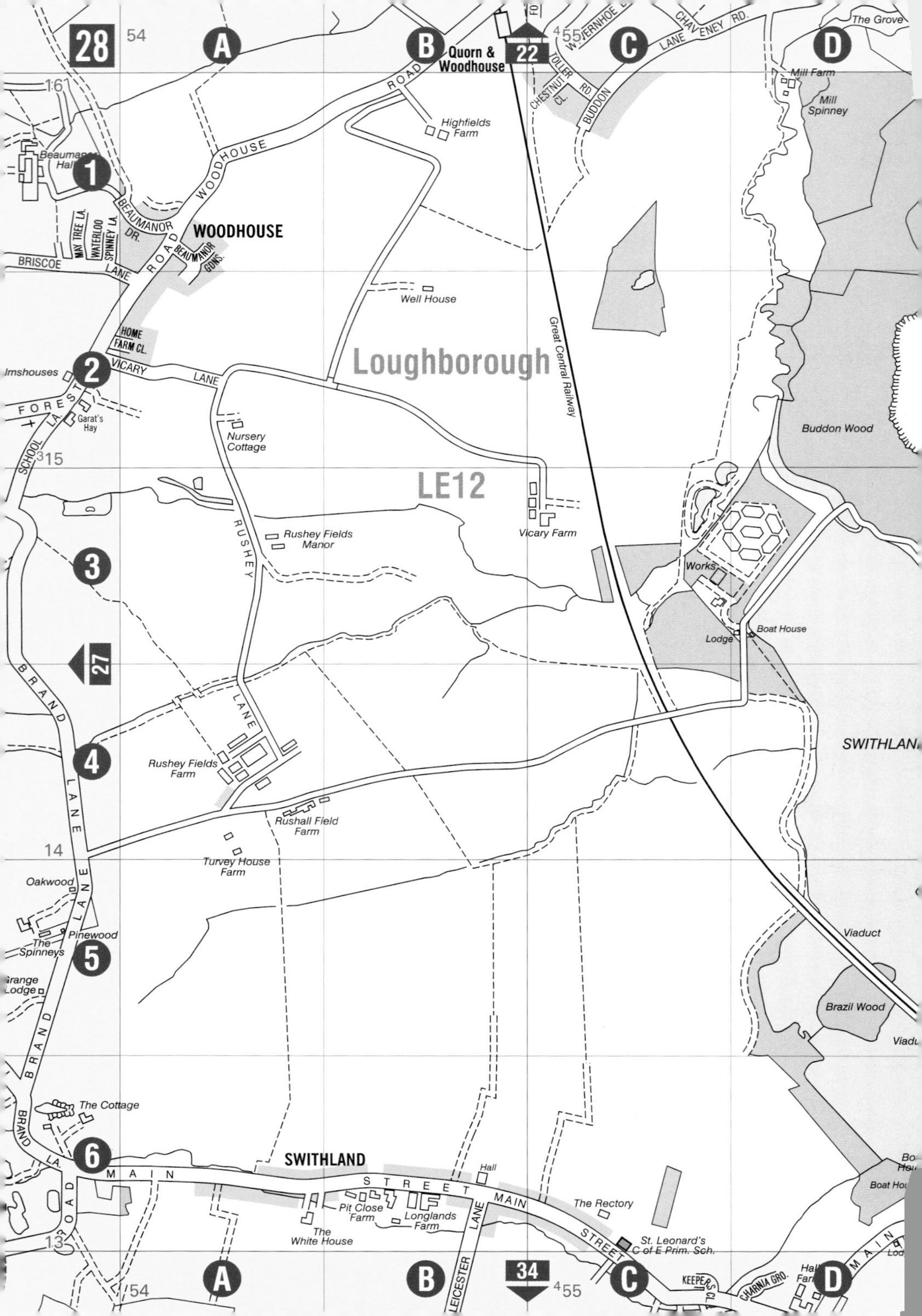
Quorn & Woodhouse
22
WOODHOUSE
Beaumanor Hall
BEAUMANOR DR.
MAY TREE LA.
WATERLOO
SPINNEY LA.
BRISCOE LANE
WOODHOUSE ROAD
BEAUMANOR GDNS.
HOME FARM CL.
VICARY LANE
FOREST ST.
Almshouses
Garat's Hay
SCHOOL LA.
Highfields Farm
Well House
Loughborough
Nursery Cottage
LE12
Rushey Fields Manor
Vicary Farm
RUSHEY LANE
Great Central Railway
W. JERNHOE
CHAVENEY RD.
BUDDON LANE
TOLLER RD.
CHESTNUT CL.
The Grove
Mill Farm
Mill Spinney
Buddon Wood
Works
Lodge
Boat House
SWITHLAND
27
BRAND LANE
Rushey Fields Farm
Rushall Field Farm
Turvey House Farm
Oakwood
Pinewood
The Spinneys
Grange Lodge
Viaduct
Brazil Wood
The Cottage
SWITHLAND
MAIN STREET
Hall
Pit Close Farm
Longlands Farm
The White House
The Rectory
St. Leonard's C of E Prim. Sch.
LEICESTER LANE
ROAD
KEEPERS CL.
CHARNIA GRO.
MAIN
34
54
55
14
13
15
A
B
C
D
1
2
3
4
5
6

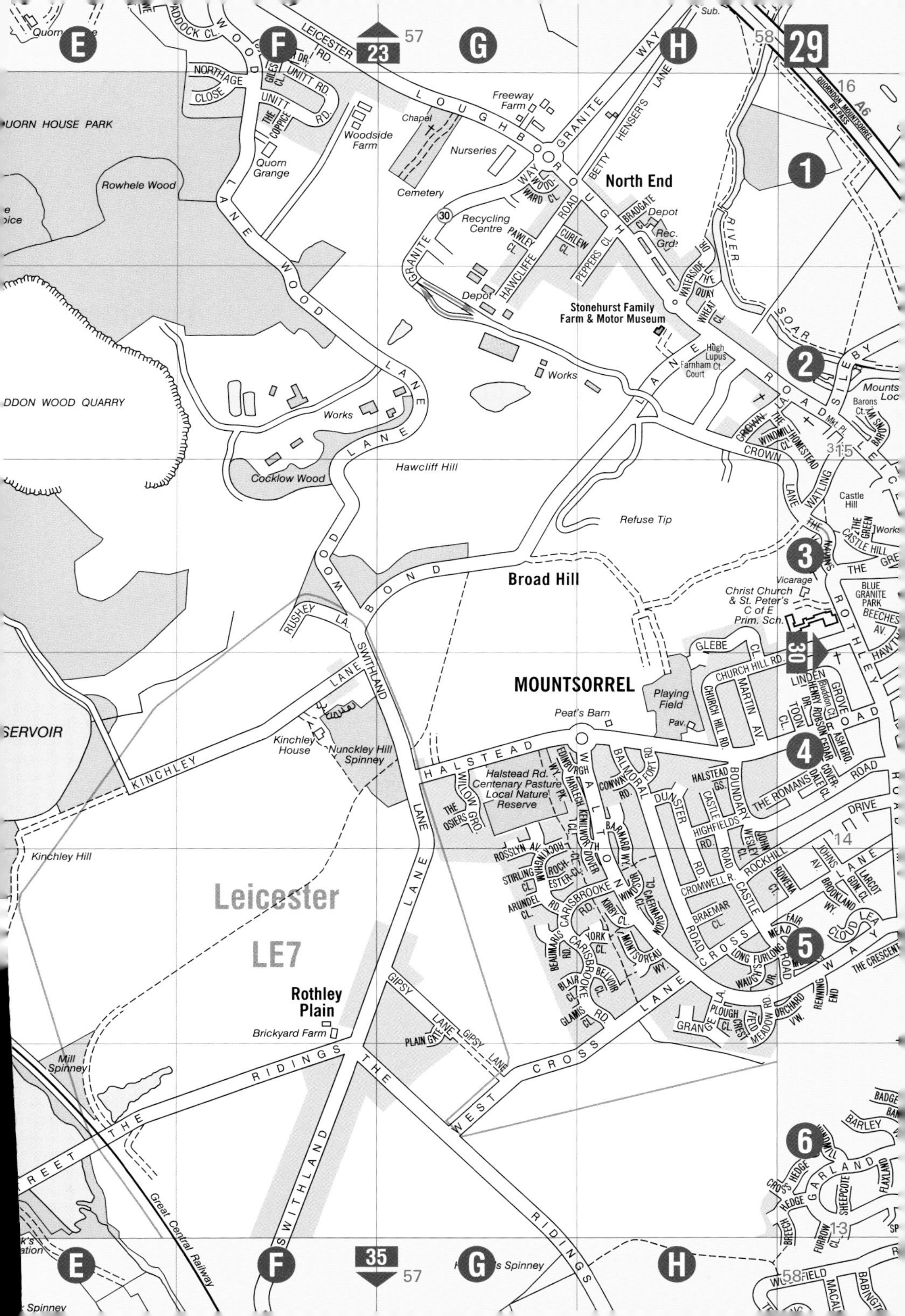

29
23
57
35
58
E
F
G
H
1
2
3
4
5
6
MOUNTSORREL
North End
Broad Hill
Rothley Plain
Leicester
LE7
Quorn House Park
Rowhele Wood
Quorn Grange
Woodside Farm
Freeway Farm
Chapel
Nurseries
Cemetery
Recycling Centre
Depot
Rec. Grd.
Stonehurst Family Farm & Motor Museum
Works
Hugh Lupus
Farnham Ct.
Farnham Court
Hawcliff Hill
Cocklow Wood
Refuse Tip
Castle Hill
Vicarage
Christ Church & St. Peter's C of E Prim. Sch.
Blue Granite Park
Playing Field
Pav.
Peat's Barn
Kinchley House
Nunckley Hill Spinney
Kinchley Hill
Halstead Rd. Centenary Pasture Local Nature Reserve
Brickyard Farm
Mill Spinney
Great Central Railway
Barons Ct.
Mkt. Pl.
Loughborough Road
Granite Way
Leicester Rd.
Wood Lane
Bond Lane
Swithland Lane
Kinchley Lane
Rushey La.
Halstead Road
Walton Way
Cross Lane
West Cross Lane
Gipsy Lane
The Ridings
Street
Crown Lane
Rothley Road
Sileby Road
Soar Lane
River Soar
Quorndon Mountsorrel By-Pass
A6
Betty Henser's Lane
Northage Close
Unitt Rd.
Giles Cl.
The Coppice
Woodward Cl.
Pawley Cl.
Curlew Cl.
Hawcliffe Rd.
Peppers Cl.
Bradgate Cl.
Waterside Dr.
The Quay
Wheat Cl.
Windmill Cl.
The Homestead
Watling St.
The Green
Castle Hill
Beeches Av.
Glebe Cl.
Church Hill Rd.
Martin Av.
Linden Grove
Buddon Cl.
Henry Robson Dr.
Toon Cl.
Cedar Rd.
Ash Gro.
The Romans
Dale Cl.
Coverdale
Halstead Gs.
Castle Highfields
Boundary Rd.
Wesley Cl.
John St.
Rockhill Dr.
Johns Av.
Larcot Gdn. Cl.
Brookland Wy.
Cloud Lea
Fair Mead
Rowena Ct.
Cromwell Rd.
Castle Rd.
Braemar Cl.
Long Furlong
Waugh's Dr.
Mead Road
Plough Cl.
Field Crest
Meadow Rd.
Orchard Vw.
Renning End
The Crescent
Grange La.
Dunster Rd.
Balmoral Rd.
Fort Rd.
Conway Rd.
Edinburgh Wy.
Harlech Cl.
Kenilworth Cl.
Dover Cl.
Barnard Wy.
Windsor Cl.
Caernarvon Cl.
Kirby Cl.
Montsoreau Wy.
York Cl.
Carisbrooke Rd.
Rosslyn Av.
Rockingham Cl.
Rochester Cl.
Stirling Cl.
Arundel Cl.
Beaumaris Rd.
Blair Cl.
Belvoir Cl.
Glamis Cl.
The Osiers
Willow Gro.
Plain Gate
Barley Way
Windmill
Garland
Cross Hedge
Sheepcote
Flaxland
Furrow Cl.
Beech Hedge
Badger
Babington
Macaulay
Sub.

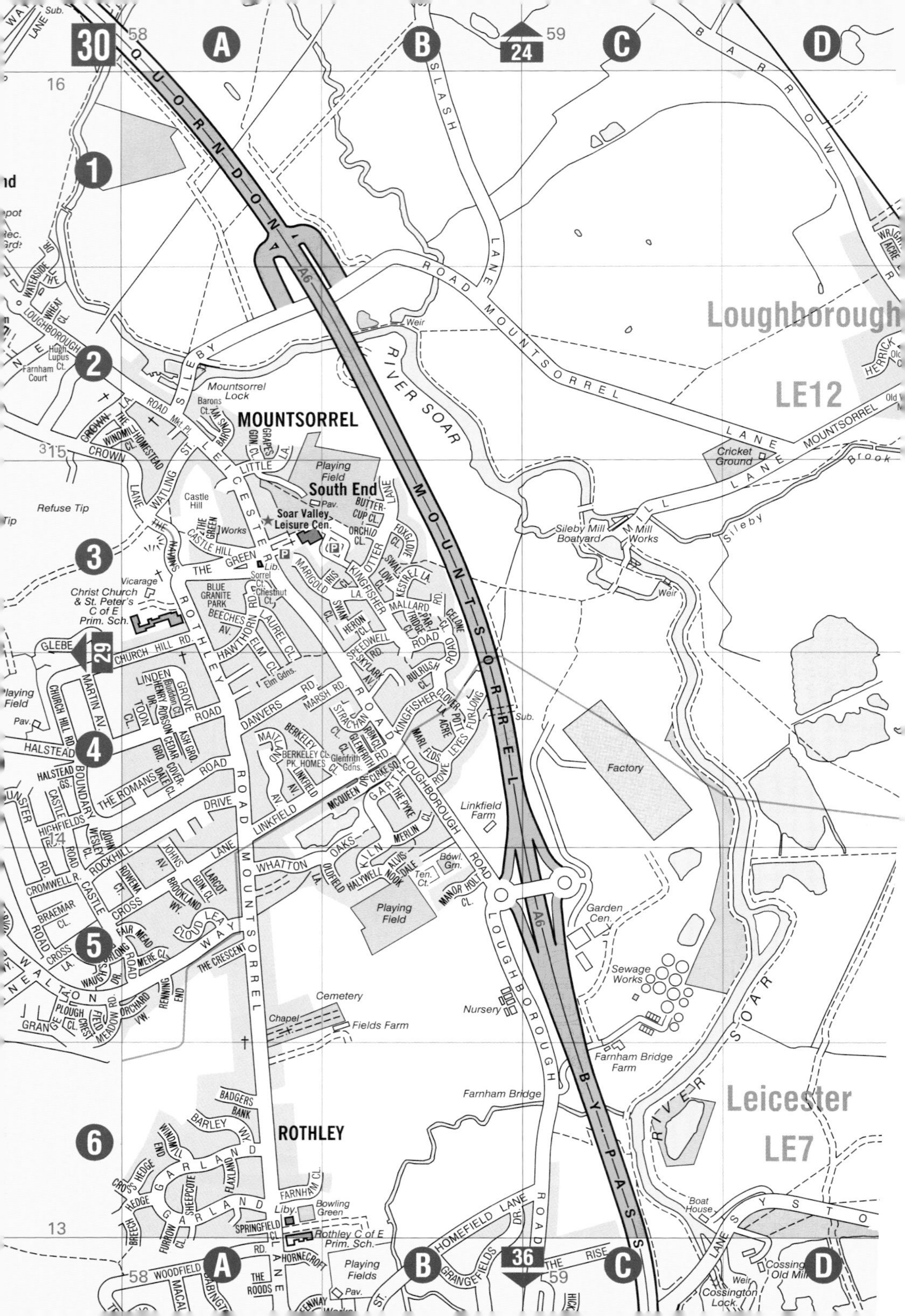
30
A
B
C
D
24
29
36
58
59
16
15
14
13
1
2
3
4
5
6
MOUNTSORREL
South End
ROTHLEY
Loughborough
LE12
Leicester
LE7
QUORNDON
MOUNTSORREL
BY PASS
A6
RIVER SOAR
Soar Valley Leisure Cen.
Castle Hill
Refuse Tip
Mountsorrel Lock
Christ Church & St. Peter's C of E Prim. Sch.
Vicarage
Blue Granite Park
Playing Field
Cricket Ground
Sileby Mill Boatyard
Mill Works
Weir
Factory
Linkfield Farm
Garden Cen.
Sewage Works
Nursery
Cemetery
Chapel
Fields Farm
Farnham Bridge Farm
Farnham Bridge
Boat House
Cossington Lock
Cossington Old Mill
Rothley C of E Prim. Sch.
Bowling Green
Playing Fields
Liby.
Lib.
Works
Pav.
Sub.
Bowl. Grn.
Ten. Ct.
Mkt. Pl.
SLASH LANE
BARROW ROAD
MOUNTSORREL LANE
MILL LANE
SILEBY ROAD
LOUGHBOROUGH ROAD
LEICESTER ROAD
MOUNTSORREL LANE
ROTHLEY ROAD
WATLING ST.
CROWN LANE
CHURCH HILL RD.
HALSTEAD RD.
BOUNDARY ROAD
CASTLE ROAD
ROCKHILL DRIVE
LINKFIELD ROAD
WHATTON OAKS
CROSS LANE
WALTON LANE
GARLAND
HOMEFIELD LANE
GRANGEFIELDS DR.
THE RISE
SYSTON LANE
Sileby Brook

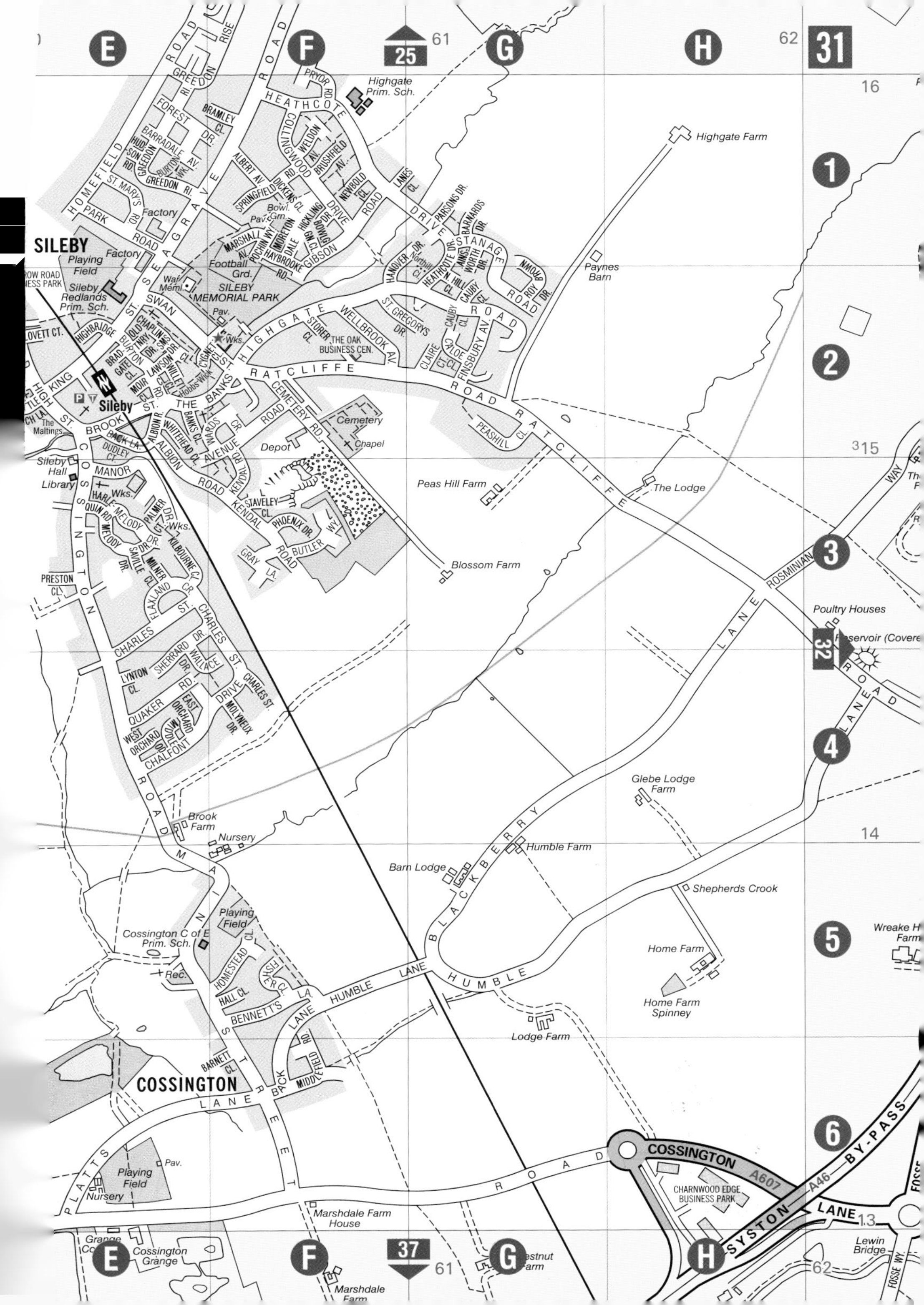

Highgate Farm

SILEBY

Highgate Prim. Sch.

Paynes Barn

The Lodge

Peas Hill Farm

Blossom Farm

Poultry Houses

Reservoir (Covered)

32

Glebe Lodge Farm

Humble Farm

Barn Lodge

Shepherds Crook

Wreake H Farm

Home Farm

Home Farm Spinney

Lodge Farm

Brook Farm

Nursery

Cossington C of E Prim. Sch.

Playing Field

Rec.

COSSINGTON

COSSINGTON

CHARNWOOD EDGE BUSINESS PARK

Marshdale Farm House

Cossington Grange

Lewin Bridge

Chestnut Farm

Grange

Marshdale Farm

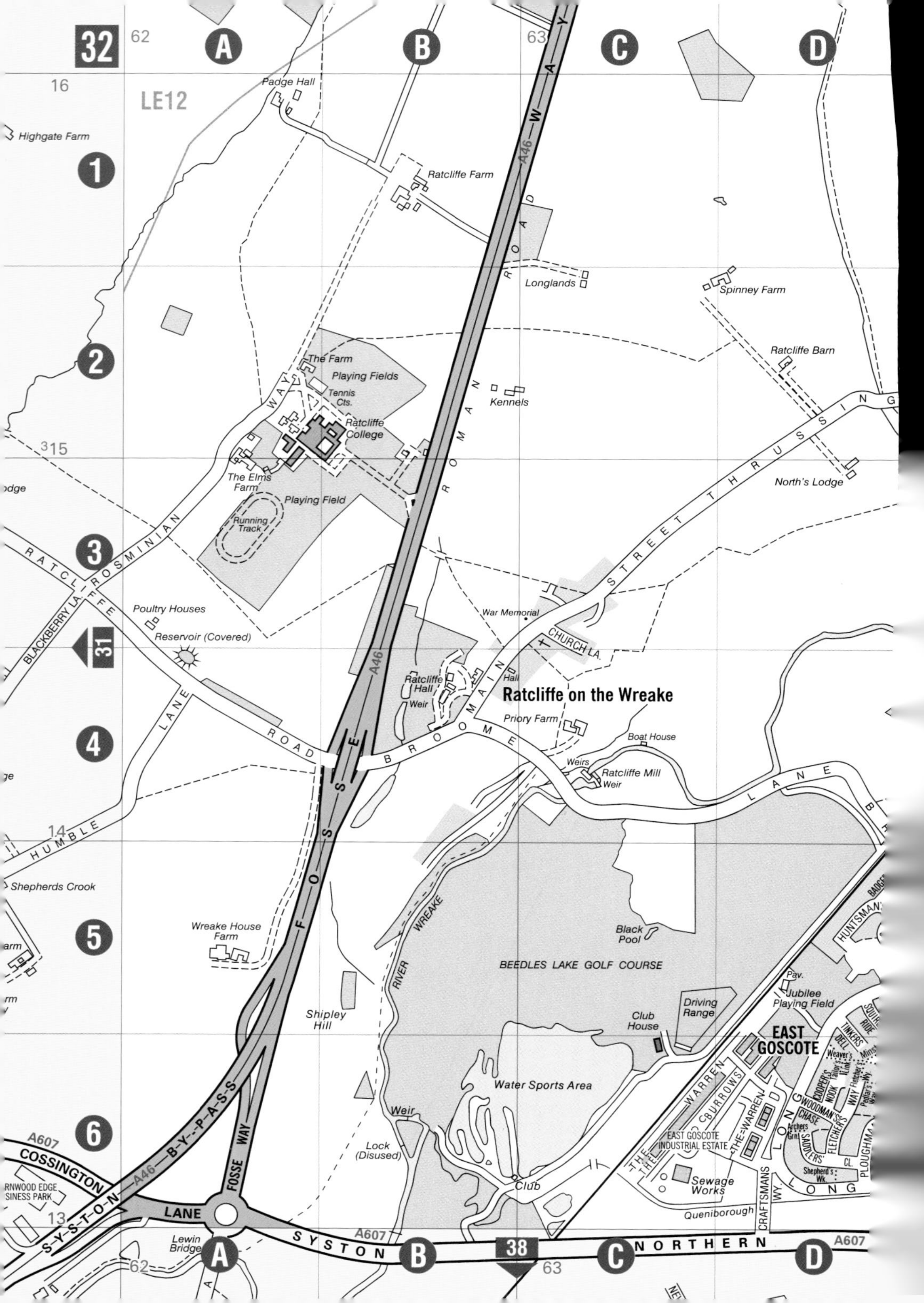

62   **A**   **B**   63   **C**   **D**

16

LE12

Highgate Farm

Padge Hall

1

Ratcliffe Farm

Longlands

Spinney Farm

Ratcliffe Barn

2

The Farm
Playing Fields

Tennis
Cts.

Kennels

Ratcliffe
College

315

North's Lodge

The Elms
Farm

odge

Playing Field

Running
Track

3

Ratcliffe

Rosminian

Blackberry La.

Poultry Houses

Reservoir (Covered)

◀ **31**

War Memorial

CHURCH LA.

Street Thrussing

Ratcliffe
Hall

Lane

Ratcliffe
Hall

Ratcliffe on the Wreake

Weir

Road

Priory Farm

4

Boat House

ge

Weirs   Ratcliffe Mill

Weir

Lane

14

Humble

Shepherds Crook

5

Wreake House
Farm

River Wreake

Black
Pool

arm

BEEDLES LAKE GOLF COURSE

HUNTSMANS

rm

Pav.

Jubilee
Playing Field

Shipley
Hill

Driving
Range

EAST
GOSCOTE

Club
House

Water Sports Area

WARREN   GURRONS

THE WARREN

WOODMAN

SOUTH

INKER

Weaver's

Archers

A607   Weir

6

COSSINGTON

A46—B—Y—P—A—S—S

FOSSE WAY

Lock
(Disused)

EAST GOSCOTE
INDUSTRIAL ESTATE

Club

Sewage
Works

FLETCHERS

LONG   PLOUGHMAN

CRAFTSMANS   WY.

Shepherd's
Wk.

RNWOOD EDGE
SINESS PARK

13

SYSTON

LANE

Lewin
Bridge

SYSTON

A607   NORTHERN   A607

A   **B**   **38**   **C**   **D**

62   63

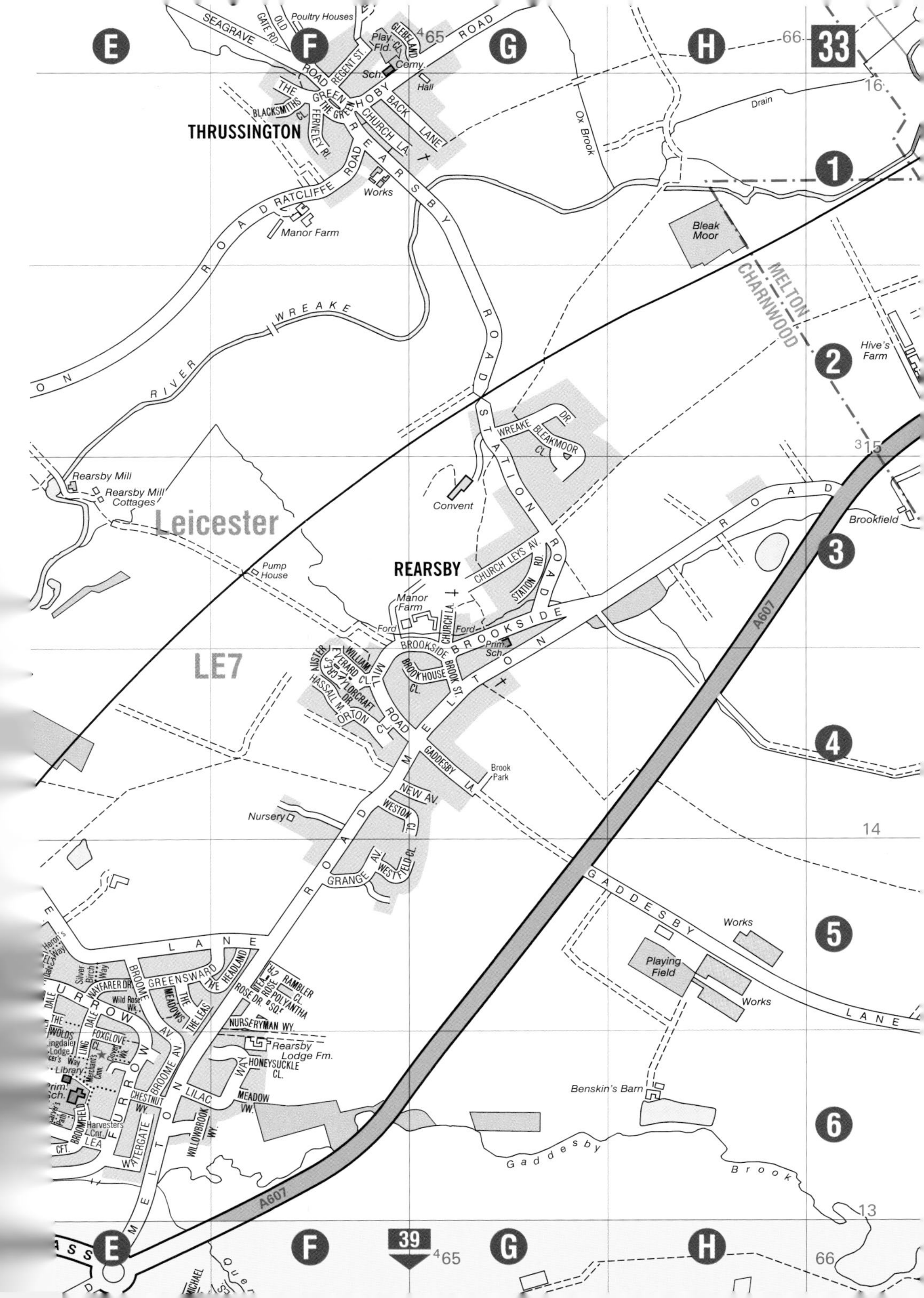
THRUSSINGTON
REARSBY
Leicester
LE7
Seagrave Road
Hoby Road
Rearsby Road
Ratcliffe Road
River Wreake
Station Road
Brookside
Melton Road
Mill Road
Gaddesby Lane
A607
Melton
Charnwood
Bleak Moor
Hive's Farm
Brookfield
Manor Farm
Works
Rearsby Mill
Rearsby Mill Cottages
Pump House
Convent
Nursery
Brook Park
Playing Field
Benskin's Barn
Rearsby Lodge Fm.
Gaddesby Brook
Ox Brook
Drain
Poultry Houses
Cemy.
Hall
Play. Fld.
Sch.
Prim. Sch.
Library
Ford
Lane
Furrow
Broome Av.
Chestnut Wy.
Watergate
Willowbrook Wy.
Lilac Way
Meadow Vw.
Honeysuckle Cl.
Nurseryman Wy.
Rose Dr.
Polyantha Sq.
Rambler Cl.
Greensward
The Headland
The Leas
The Meadows
Wayfarer Dr.
Foxglove Cl.
Lingdale
The Wolds
Harvesters Cnr.
Broomfield
Grange Av.
Westfield Cl.
Weston Cl.
New Av.
Orton Cl.
Lorcraft
Hassall Dr.
Everard Cl.
William
Brookhouse Cl.
Brook St.
Church La.
Church Leys Av.
Station Rd.
Wreake Dr.
Bleakmoor Cl.
The Green
Blacksmiths Cl.
Ferneley Ri.
Church La.
Back Lane
Regent St.
Gleneland Cl.
Old Gate Rd.
E F G H
1 2 3 4 5 6
465
66
16
15
14
13
39

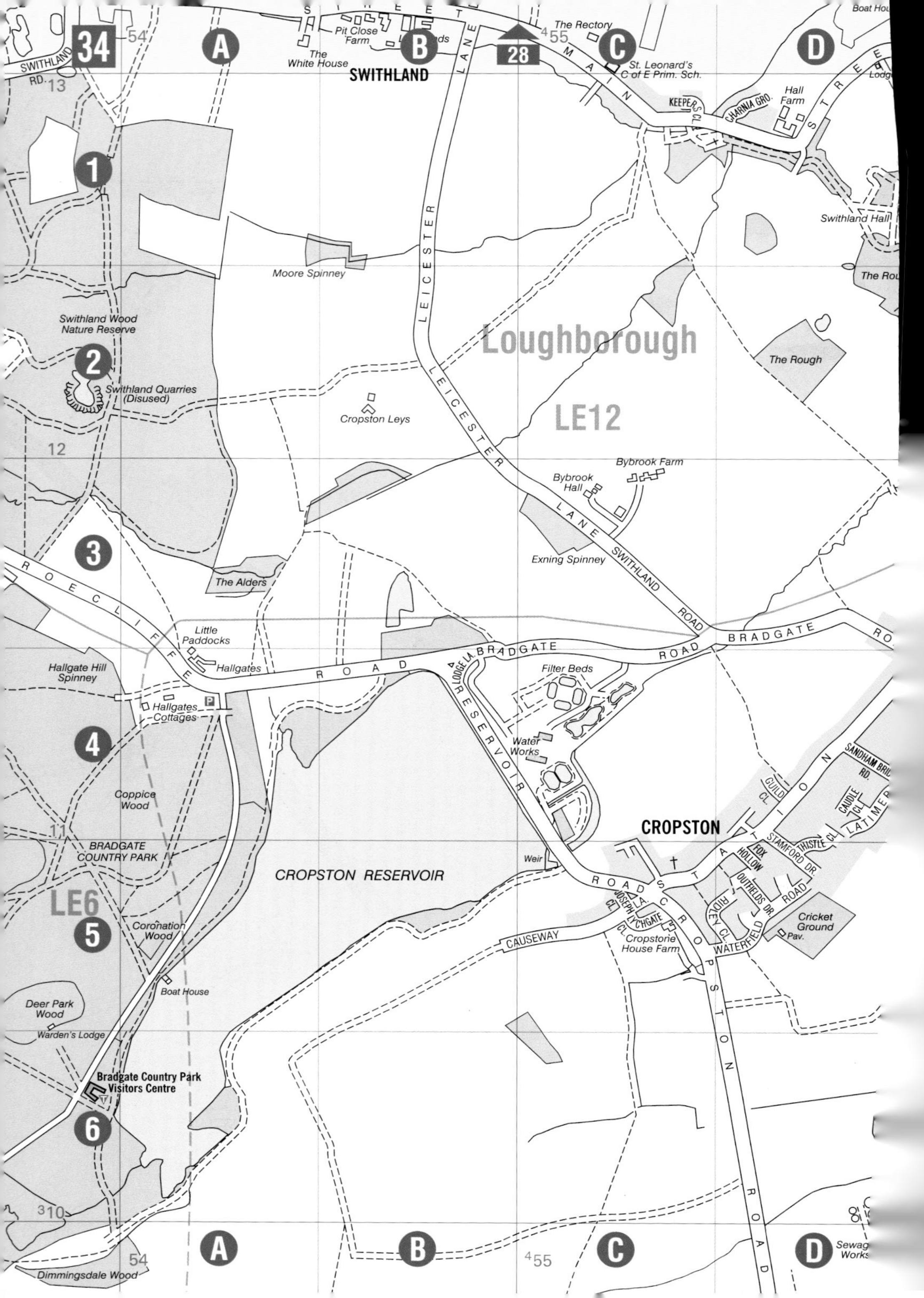

28
SWITHLAND
Pit Close Farm
The White House
The Rectory
St. Leonard's C of E Prim. Sch.
MAIN STREET
SWITHLAND RD.
KEEPERS CL.
CHARNIA GRO.
Hall Farm
Swithland Hall
The Rough
Moore Spinney
LEICESTER LANE
Loughborough
LE12
Swithland Wood Nature Reserve
Swithland Quarries (Disused)
Cropston Leys
Bybrook Farm
Bybrook Hall
Exning Spinney
SWITHLAND ROAD
The Alders
ROECLIFFE ROAD
Little Paddocks
Hallgates
Hallgate Hill Spinney
Hallgates Cottages
BRADGATE ROAD
LODGE LA.
Filter Beds
Water Works
RESERVOIR ROAD
Coppice Wood
BRADGATE COUNTRY PARK
CROPSTON RESERVOIR
Weir
CROPSTON
STATION ROAD
GUILD CL.
SANDHAM BRIDGE RD.
CAUDLE CL.
LATIMER
STAMFORD DR.
THISTLE CL.
FOX HOLLOW
OUTHIELDS DR.
RIDLEY CL.
WATERFIELD
Cricket Ground
Pav.
LE6
Coronation Wood
CAUSEWAY
JOSEPH CL.
LYCHGATE CL.
Cropstone House Farm
CROPSTON ROAD
Boat House
Deer Park Wood
Warden's Lodge
Bradgate Country Park Visitors Centre
Dimmingsdale Wood
Sewage Works

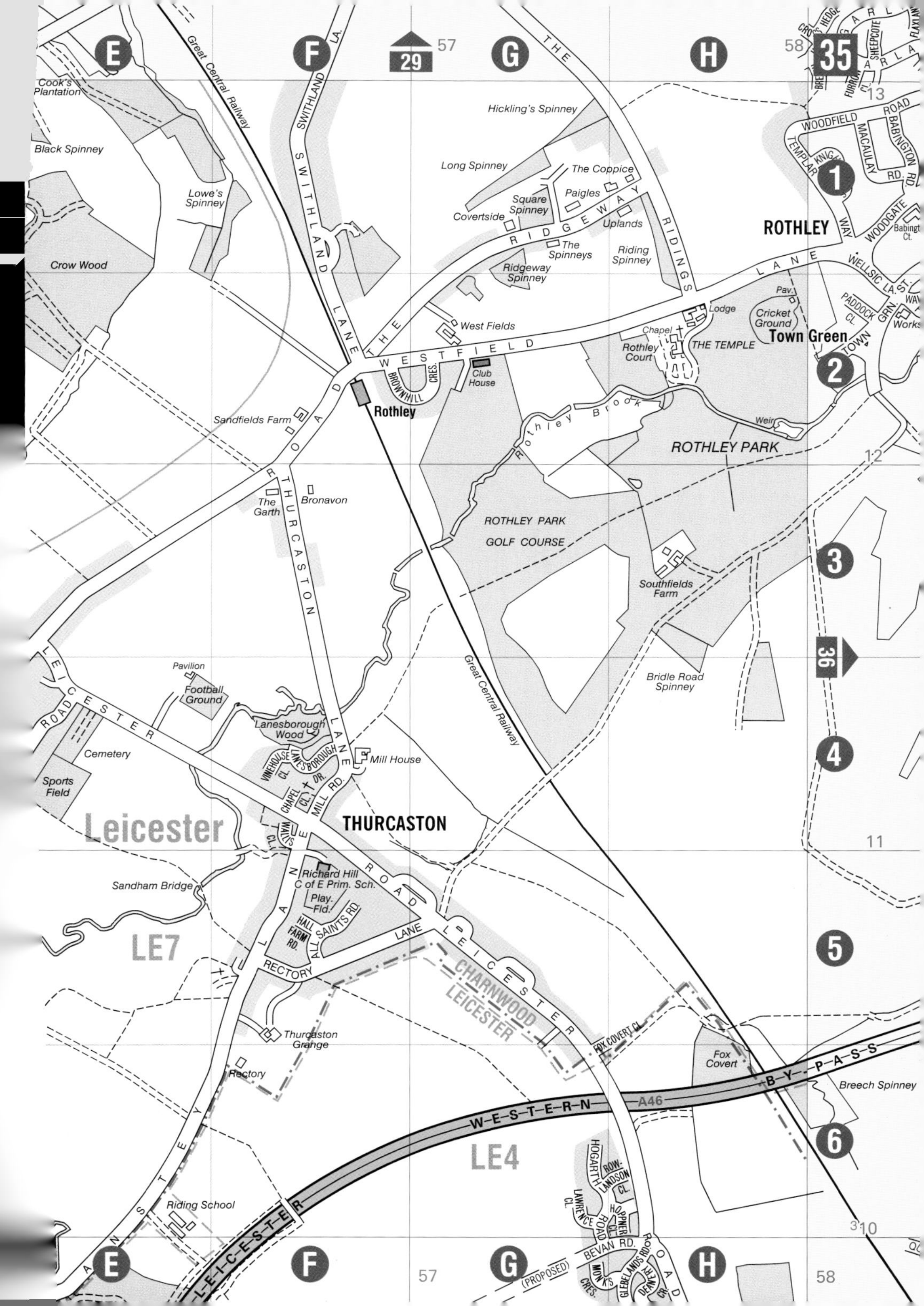
E
F
G
H
29
57
58
Cook's Plantation
Great Central Railway
Swithland La.
The Ridings
Hickling's Spinney
Black Spinney
Long Spinney
The Coppice
Lowe's Spinney
Square Spinney
Paigles
Covertside
Ridgeway
Uplands
The Spinneys
Riding Spinney
Crow Wood
Ridgeway Spinney
Rothley
Lane
Woodfield Road
Templar Way
Macaulay
Babington Rd.
Woodgate
Wellsic La.
Paddock Cl.
Town Green
Works
Cricket Ground
Pav.
Lodge
Chapel
The Temple
Rothley Court
West Fields
The Westfield
Brownhill Cres.
Club House
Swithland Lane
Road
Sandfields Farm
Rothley Brook
Weir
Rothley Park
The Garth
Bronavon
Rothley Park Golf Course
Southfields Farm
Thurcaston Lane
Bridle Road Spinney
Pavilion
Football Ground
Leicester Road
Lanesborough Wood
Cemetery
Mill House
Sports Field
Vinehouse Cl.
Lanesborough Dr.
Chapel Cl.
Mill Rd.
Leicester
Thurcaston
Walls Cl.
Sandham Bridge
Richard Hill C of E Prim. Sch.
Play. Fld.
Hall Farm Rd.
All Saints Rd
Lane
LE7
Rectory
Charnwood
Leicester
Fox Covert Cl.
Fox Covert
Thurcaston Grange
Rectory
Breech Spinney
A46
Western By-Pass
LE4
Hogarth Row
Landson Cl.
Lawrence Cl.
Hoppner Cl.
Riding School
Anstey Lane
Leicester
Bevan Rd.
(Proposed)
Monks Cres.
Glebelands Road
Deanery Cr.
Road
1
2
3
4
5
6
36
13
12
11
10

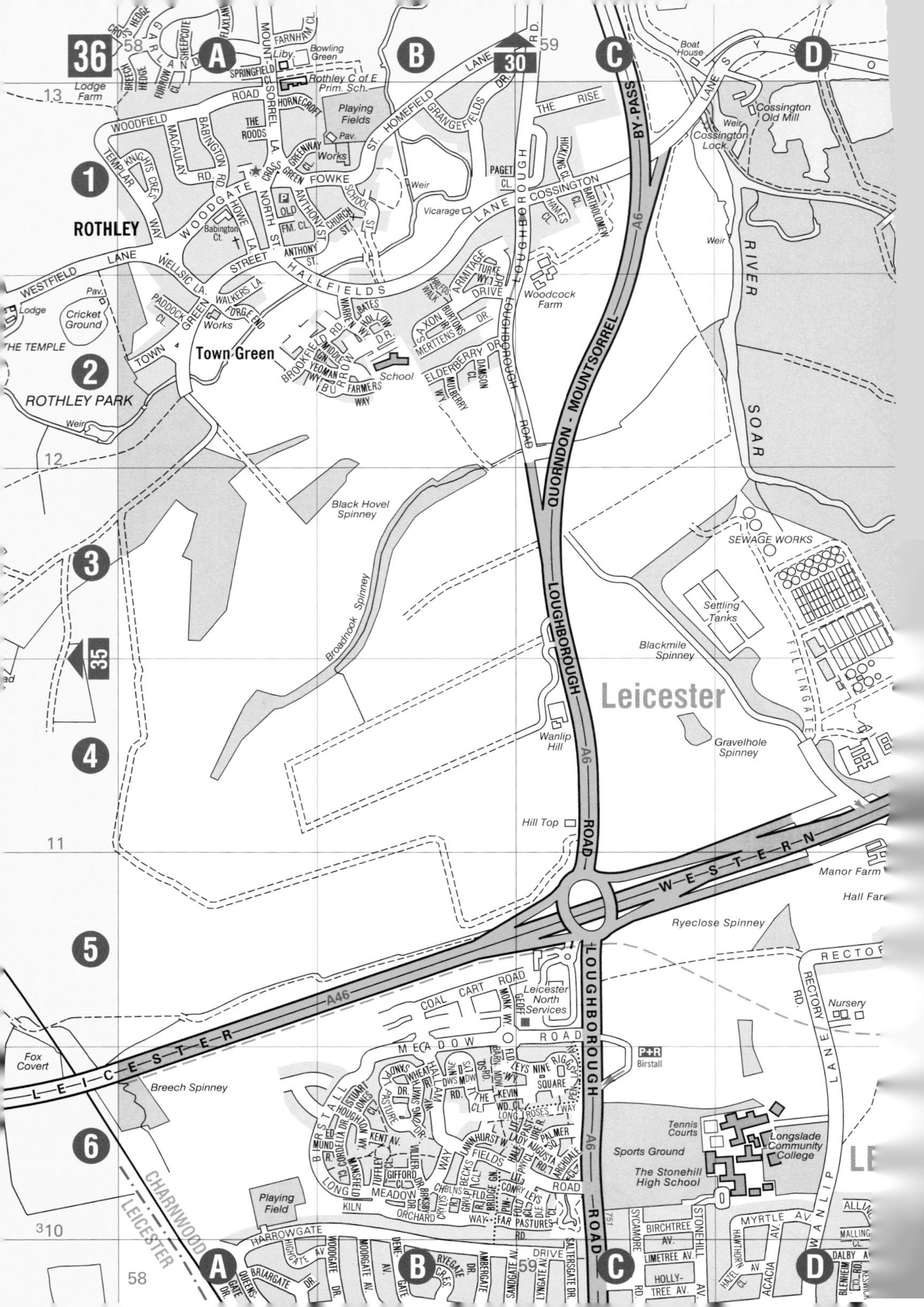
36
30
35
A
B
C
D
1
2
3
4
5
6
58
59
13
12
11
10
ROTHLEY
Town Green
ROTHLEY PARK
THE TEMPLE
Lodge Farm
Lodge
Cricket Ground
Pav.
Weir
WOODFIELD ROAD
TEMPLAR WAY
KNIGHTS CRES.
MACAULAY RD.
BABINGTON RD.
THE ROODS
SORREL LA.
MOUNTSORREL LA.
HORNECROFT
SPRINGFIELD CL.
FARNHAM CL.
Liby.
Bowling Green
Rothley C of E Prim. Sch.
Playing Fields
Pav.
Works
GREENWAY CL.
CROSS GREEN
FOWKE ST.
SCHOOL ST.
HOMEFIELD LANE
GRANGEFIELDS DR.
THE RISE
HICKLING CL.
PAGET CL.
WOODGATE
HOWE LA.
NORTH ST.
OLD FM. CL.
ANTHONY ST.
CHURCH ST.
Babington Ct.
WESTFIELD LANE
WELLSIC LA.
STREET
HALLFIELDS
Vicarage
COSSINGTON LANE
HAMES CL.
BARTHOLOMEW
LOUGHBOROUGH ROAD
ARMITAGE DRIVE
TURKEY WY.
Woodcock Farm
WALKERS LA.
FORGE END
PADDOCK CL.
TOWN GREEN
Works
WARREN WY.
BATES CL.
HOLLOW DR.
BROOKFIELD RD.
MIDDLE GN.
YEOMAN WY
FARMERS WAY
School
SAXON DR.
MERTTENS DR.
BURTONS
ELDERBERRY DR.
DAMSON CL.
MULBERRY WY.
QUORNDON - MOUNTSORREL BY-PASS
A6
Boat House
Cossington Old Mill
Cossington Lock
RIVER SOAR
Black Hovel Spinney
Broadnook Spinney
SEWAGE WORKS
Settling Tanks
Blackmile Spinney
FILLINGATE
Leicester
Wanlip Hill
Gravelhole Spinney
Hill Top
WESTERN
Manor Farm
Hall Farm
Ryeclose Spinney
RECTORY RD.
RECTORY LANE
Nursery
A46
LEICESTER
COAL CART ROAD
MONK WY.
GEOFF
Leicester North Services
MEADOW ROAD
P+R Birstall
Fox Covert
Breech Spinney
BIRSTALL
STUART
HOUGHTON WY.
KENT AV.
PASTURE
HALLAM
SQUARE
KEVIN
LADY AUGUSTA
PALMER
LAWNHURST
FIELDS
LONG MEADOW
MANSFIELD
TUFFLEY
GIFFORD CL.
KILN
ORCHARD WAY
FAR PASTURES
ROAD
Tennis Courts
Sports Ground
Longslade Community College
The Stonehill High School
Playing Field
CHARNWOOD
HARROWGATE
HIGHGATE AV.
WOODGATE DR.
QUEENSGATE DR.
BRIARGATE DR.
MORGATE AV.
DENEGATE
RYEGATE CRES.
AMBERGATE DR.
SANDGATE AV.
LYNGATE AV.
SALTERSGATE DR.
DRIVE
SYCAMORE RD.
BIRCHTREE AV.
LIMETREE AV.
HOLLYTREE AV.
STONEHILL AV.
MYRTLE AV.
HAWTHORN AV.
HAZEL CL.
ACACIA AV.
WANLIP LANE
ALLINGTON
MALLING CL.
DALBY AV.
BLENHEIM CL.

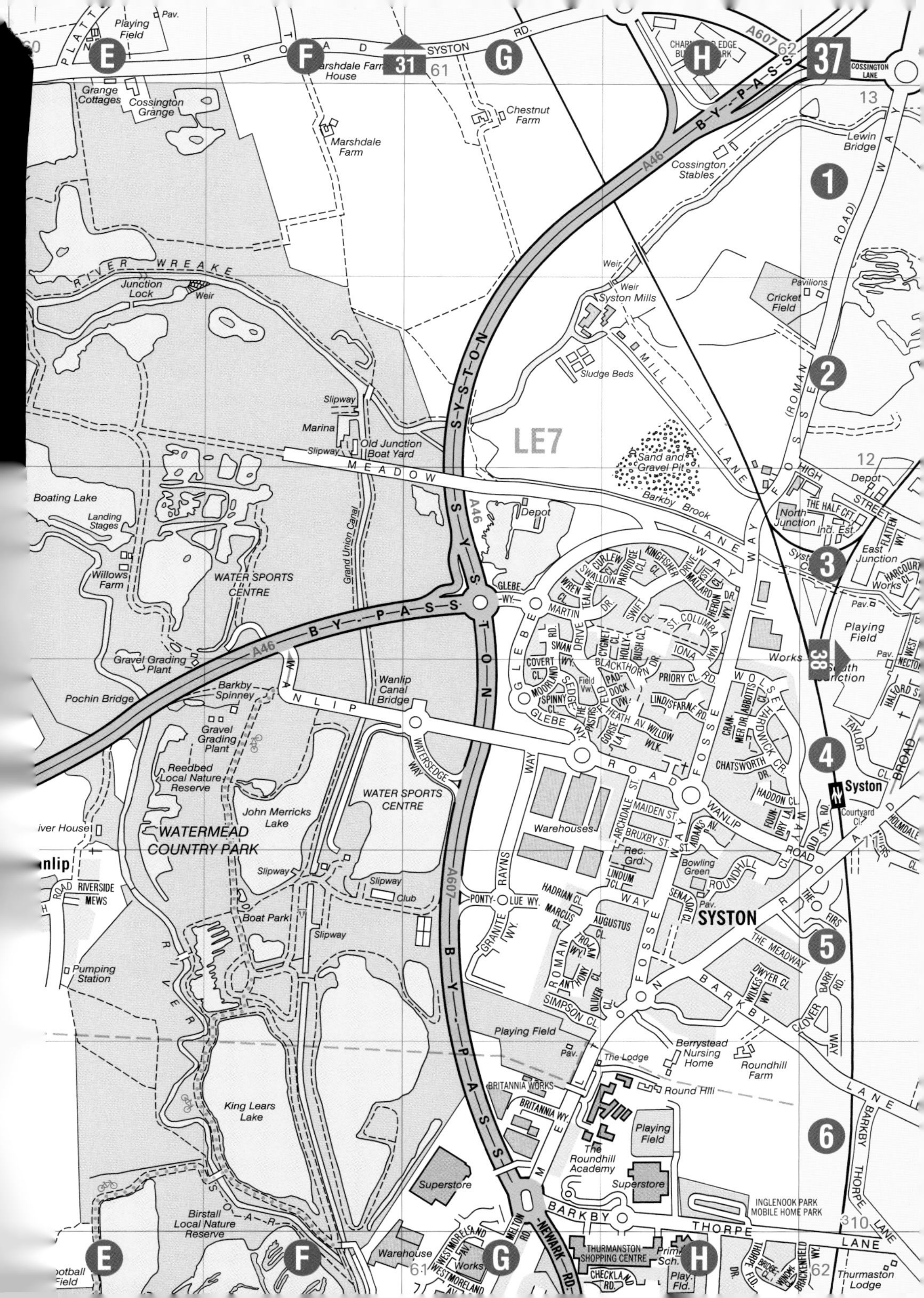

31
37
38
LE7
SYSTON
WATERMEAD COUNTRY PARK
SYSTON BY-PASS
A46
A607
Playing Field
Grange Cottages
Cossington Grange
Marshdale Farm House
Marshdale Farm
Chestnut Farm
Cossington Stables
Lewin Bridge
COSSINGTON LANE
RIVER WREAKE
Junction Lock
Weir
Syston Mills
Sludge Beds
MILL LANE
Sand and Gravel Pit
Cricket Field
Pavilions
FOSSE WAY (ROMAN ROAD)
HIGH STREET
Depot
North Junction
East Junction
South Junction
Ind. Est.
Works
Playing Field
Slipway
Marina
Old Junction Boat Yard
MEADOW LANE
Barkby Brook
Boating Lake
Landing Stages
Willows Farm
WATER SPORTS CENTRE
Grand Union Canal
Gravel Grading Plant
Pochin Bridge
Barkby Spinney
WANLIP ROAD
Wanlip Canal Bridge
Reedbed Local Nature Reserve
John Merricks Lake
Boat Park
Club
King Lears Lake
Birstall Local Nature Reserve
Pumping Station
RIVERSIDE MEWS
Warehouses
Rec. Grd.
Bowling Green
Playing Field
The Lodge
Berrystead Nursing Home
Roundhill Farm
Round Hill
BRITANNIA WORKS
BRITANNIA WY.
The Roundhill Academy
Superstore
Warehouse
INGLENOOK PARK MOBILE HOME PARK
BARKBY THORPE LANE
BARKBY LANE
THURMANSTON SHOPPING CENTRE
Prim. Sch.
Play. Fld.
Thurmaston Lodge
NEWARK RD.
MELTON RD.
WESTMORELAND AV.
CHECKLAND RD.
Syston

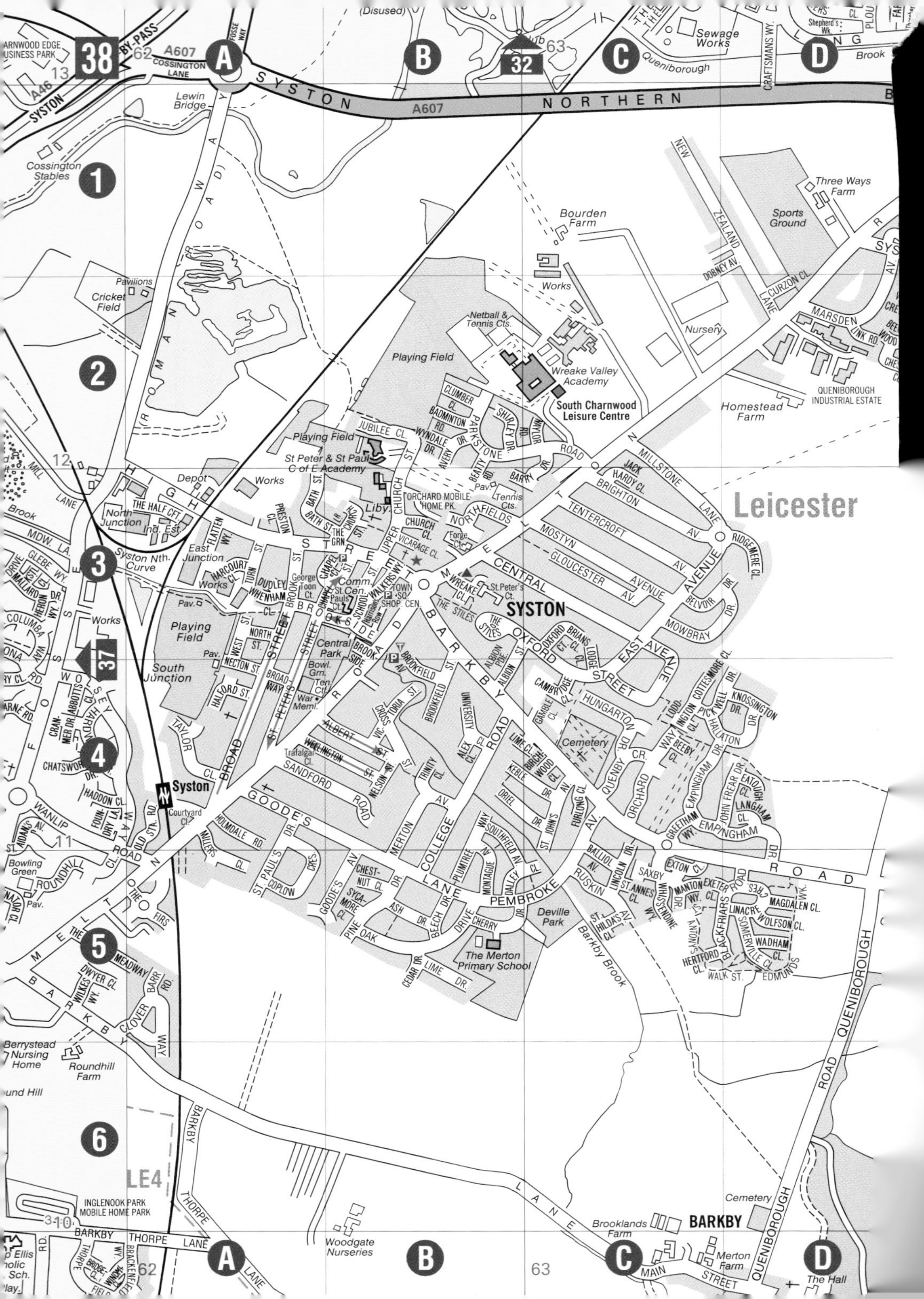

38
32
37
A
B
C
D
1
2
3
4
5
6
SYSTON NORTHERN BY-PASS
A607
A46
COSSINGTON LANE
FOSSE WAY
ROMAN ROAD
Lewin Bridge
Cossington Stables
Cricket Field
Pavilions
Sewage Works
Queniborough
CRAFTSMANS WY.
Brook
Bourden Farm
Works
Three Ways Farm
Sports Ground
NEW ZEALAND LANE
DOBNEY AV.
CURZON CL.
MARSDEN
LINK RD.
Nursery
QUENIBOROUGH INDUSTRIAL ESTATE
Homestead Farm
Netball & Tennis Cts.
Wreake Valley Academy
South Charnwood Leisure Centre
Playing Field
Leicester
SYSTON
St Peter & St Paul C of E Academy
JUBILEE CL.
WYNDALE DR.
CLUMBER CL.
BADMINTON RD.
AVERY DR.
PARKSTONE ROAD
SHIRLEY DR.
NAYLOR RD.
BEATTY RD.
BARRY DR.
Tennis Cts.
JACK HARDY CL.
MILLSTONE LANE
BRIGHTON AV.
TENTERCROFT AV.
MOSTYN AV.
GLOUCESTER AVENUE
CENTRAL AV.
RIDGEMERE CL.
EAST AVENUE
BELVOIR DR.
MOWBRAY DR.
HIGH STREET
Depot
THE HALF CFT.
North Junction
Ind. Est.
PRESTON CL.
BATH ST.
Liby.
ORCHARD MOBILE HOME PK.
NORTHFIELDS
CHURCH CL.
UPPER CHURCH ST.
VICARAGE CL.
Forge Ct.
MELTON ROAD
WREAKE CL.
St.Peter's Ct.
THE STILES
FLATTEN WY.
East Junction
Syston Nth. Curve
HARCOURT CL.
DUDLEY WHENHAM CL.
George Toon Ct.
Comm. Cen.
TOWN SQ. SHOP. CEN.
St. Pauls Ct.
BROOKSIDE
Central Park
Bowl. Grn.
Ten. Ctl.
War Meml.
Works
Pav.
South Junction
WEST ST.
NORTH ST.
NECTON ST.
HALFORD ST.
BROAD STREET
ST. PETER'S ST.
BROOK STREET
BROADWAY
BROOKFIELD AV.
BROOKFIELD ST.
UNIVERSITY
BARKBY ROAD
ALBION PDE.
ALBION ST.
OXFORD STREET
BRIANS CL.
LODGE CL.
CAMBRIDGE ST.
GAMBLE CL.
HUNGARTON DR.
Cemetery
QUENBY CR.
ORCHARD WAY
LODDINGTON WAY
COTTESMORE DR.
PICKWELL DR.
KNOSSINGTON DR.
HALLATON DR.
BEEBY CL.
EMPINGHAM DR.
JOHN FREAR DR.
EATOUGH CL.
LANGHAM CL.
GREETHAM WY.
EMPINGHAM
ROAD
VICTORIA ST.
CROSS ST.
ALBERT ST.
WELLINGTON ST.
Trafalgar Cl.
NELSON ST.
SANDFORD ROAD
TRINITY CL.
ALEX CL.
LIME CL.
BIRCHWOOD CL.
KEBLE DR.
ORIEL DR.
ST. JOHN'S AV.
FURLONG CL.
GOODE'S LANE
MERTON AV.
COLLEGE AV.
TAYLOR CL.
Syston
Courtyard Cl.
OLD STA. RD.
HOLMDALE RD.
MILLERS CL.
ST. PAUL'S DR.
COPLOW CRES.
GOODE'S AV.
CHESTNUT CL.
SYCAMORE CL.
PINE OAK
ASH DR.
BEECH DR.
CHERRY DRIVE
PLUMTREE WAY
MONTAGUE AV.
SOUTHFIELD AV.
DALLEY CL.
PEMBROKE AV.
Deville Park
The Merton Primary School
CEDAR DR.
LIME DR.
BALLIOL AV.
LINCOLN DR.
RUSKIN AV.
ST. ANNES CL.
SAXBY
WHISSENDINE WY.
ST. HILDA'S CL.
EXTON CL.
MANTON WY.
EXETER CL.
MAGDALEN CL.
LINACRE
WOLFSON CL.
WADHAM CL.
SOMERVILLE CL.
BLACKFRIARS
HERTFORD CL.
WALK ST.
EDMUNDS
Barkby Brook
QUENIBOROUGH ROAD
MELTON ROAD
THE FIRS
THE MEADWAY
DWYER CL.
WILKES WY.
BARR RD.
CLOVER WAY
BARKBY ROAD
Berrystead Nursing Home
Roundhill Farm
BARKBY LANE
LE4
INGLENOOK PARK MOBILE HOME PARK
BARKBY THORPE LANE
THORPE LANE
Woodgate Nurseries
Brooklands Farm
BARKBY
Cemetery
Merton Farm
MAIN STREET
The Hall
WOLSEY WAY
GLEBE WY.
MALLARD
HERON WY.
COLUMBA
CHATSWORTH DR.
HADDON CL.
FOUNDRY LA.
CRANMER DR.
ABBOTTS
WANLIP
ROUNDHILL CL.
Bowling Green
Pav.
MDW. LA.
MILL LANE
Brook
BROOK STREET
62
63
13
12
11
10

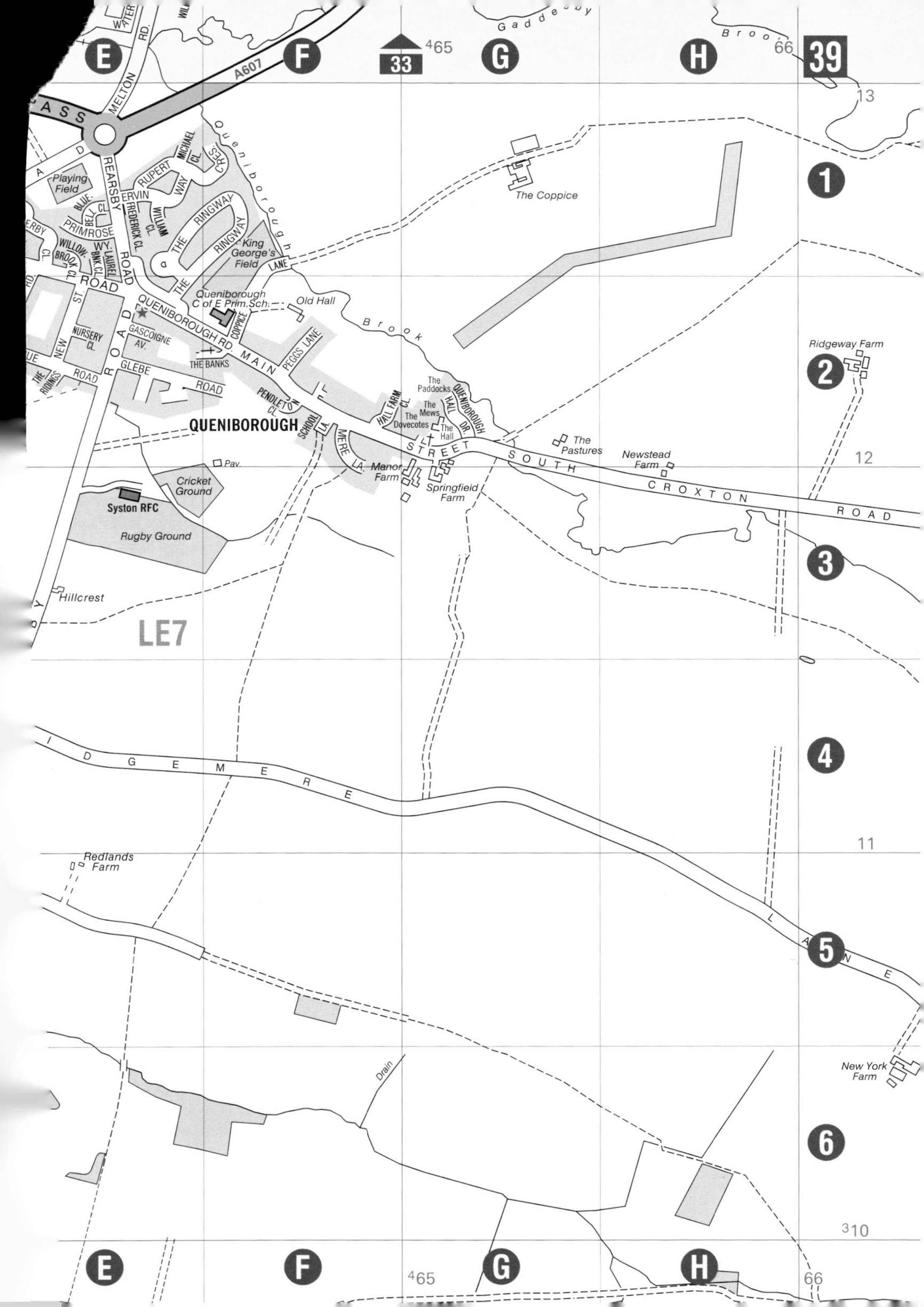

Gaddesby   Broo

1

The Coppice

2

Ridgeway Farm

12

3

4

11

5

6

310

WATER

MELTON RD
WILL...
A607
REARSBY

Queniborough
Playing Field

RUPERT WAY
MICHAEL CL
ERVIN
FREDERICK CL
WILLIAM CL
RINGWAY
The RINGWAY

King George's Field

LANE

BLUE CL
PRIMROSE
WILLOW
LAUREL
BRO...CL
NK...CL

ROAD

Queniborough RD
COPPICE

Old Hall

Brook

Queniborough
C of E Prim.Sch.

GASCOIGNE AV.
GLEBE
THE BANKS
ROAD

MAIN

PEGGS LANE

PENDLETON CL
SCHOOL LA
MERE LA.

QUENIBOROUGH

The Paddocks
The Mews
The Dovecotes
The Hall
HALL FARM CL

QUENIBOROUGH HALL DR.

STREET

The Pastures

Newstead Farm

SOUTH   CROXTON   ROAD

Pav.
Cricket Ground

Syston RFC

Rugby Ground

Manor Farm

Springfield Farm

Hillcrest

LE7

Redlands Farm

DGEMERE

LANE

New York Farm

Drain

NEW ST
NURSERY CL
THE ROUND...

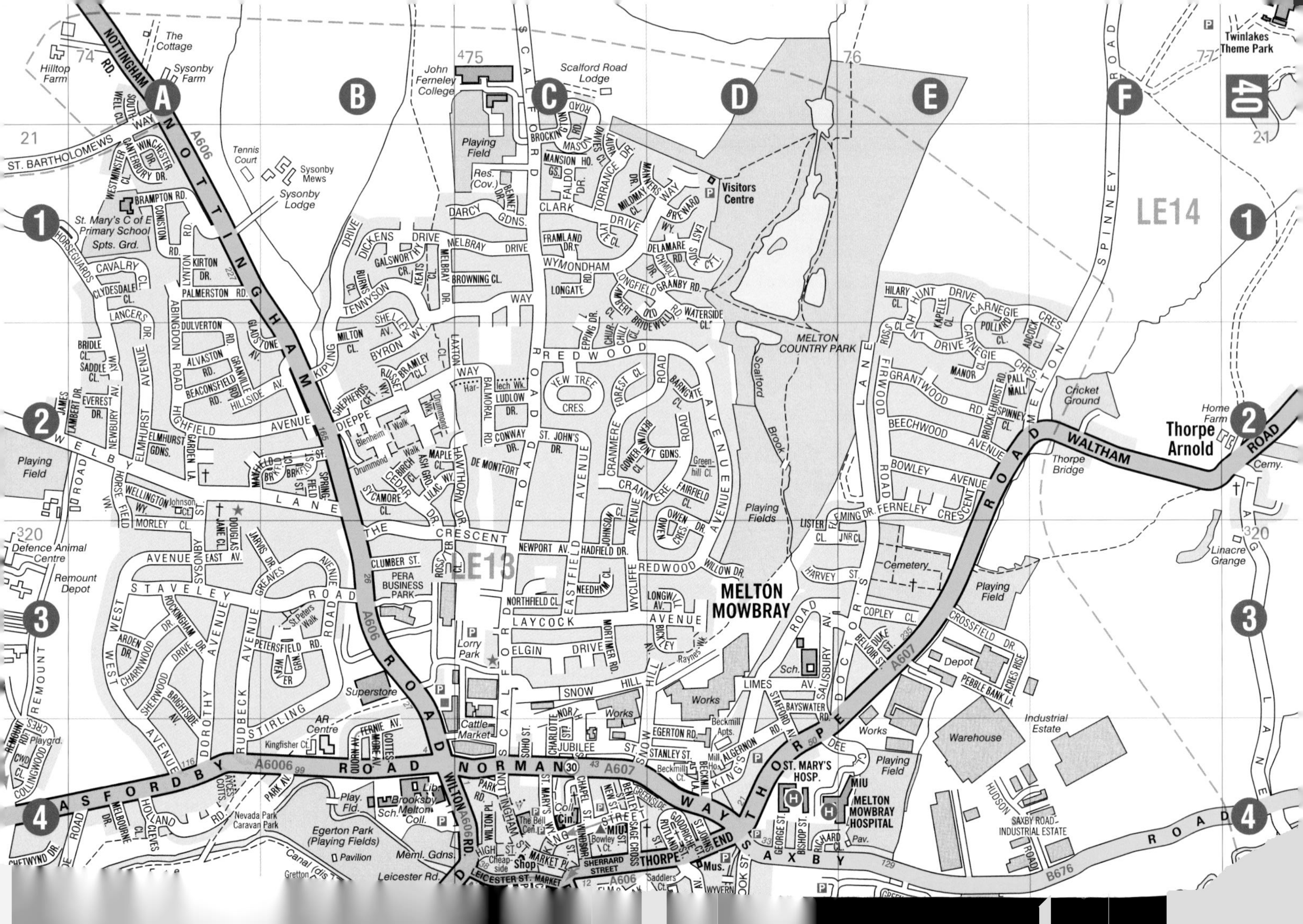

40
LE14
LE13
MELTON MOWBRAY
Thorpe Arnold
Twinlakes Theme Park
MELTON COUNTRY PARK
Visitors Centre
Scalford Brook
Playing Fields
John Ferneley College
Scalford Road Lodge
Sysonby Farm
Sysonby Lodge
Sysonby Mews
The Cottage
Hilltop Farm
St. Mary's C of E Primary School
Defence Animal Centre
Remount Depot
Cattle Market
Lorry Park
PERA BUSINESS PARK
Superstore
Industrial Estate
SAXBY ROAD INDUSTRIAL ESTATE
Warehouse
Depot
Works
Cemetery
Cricket Ground
Thorpe Bridge
Linacre Grange
Home Farm
MELTON MOWBRAY HOSPITAL
ST. MARY'S HOSP.
Egerton Park (Playing Fields)
Nevada Park Caravan Park
Brooksby Melton Coll.
NOTTINGHAM RD.
WALTHAM ROAD
SCALFORD ROAD
SPINNEY ROAD
ASFORDBY ROAD
NORMAN WAY
THORPE END
SAXBY ROAD
WILTON RD.
WELBY LANE
A606
A607
A6006
B676

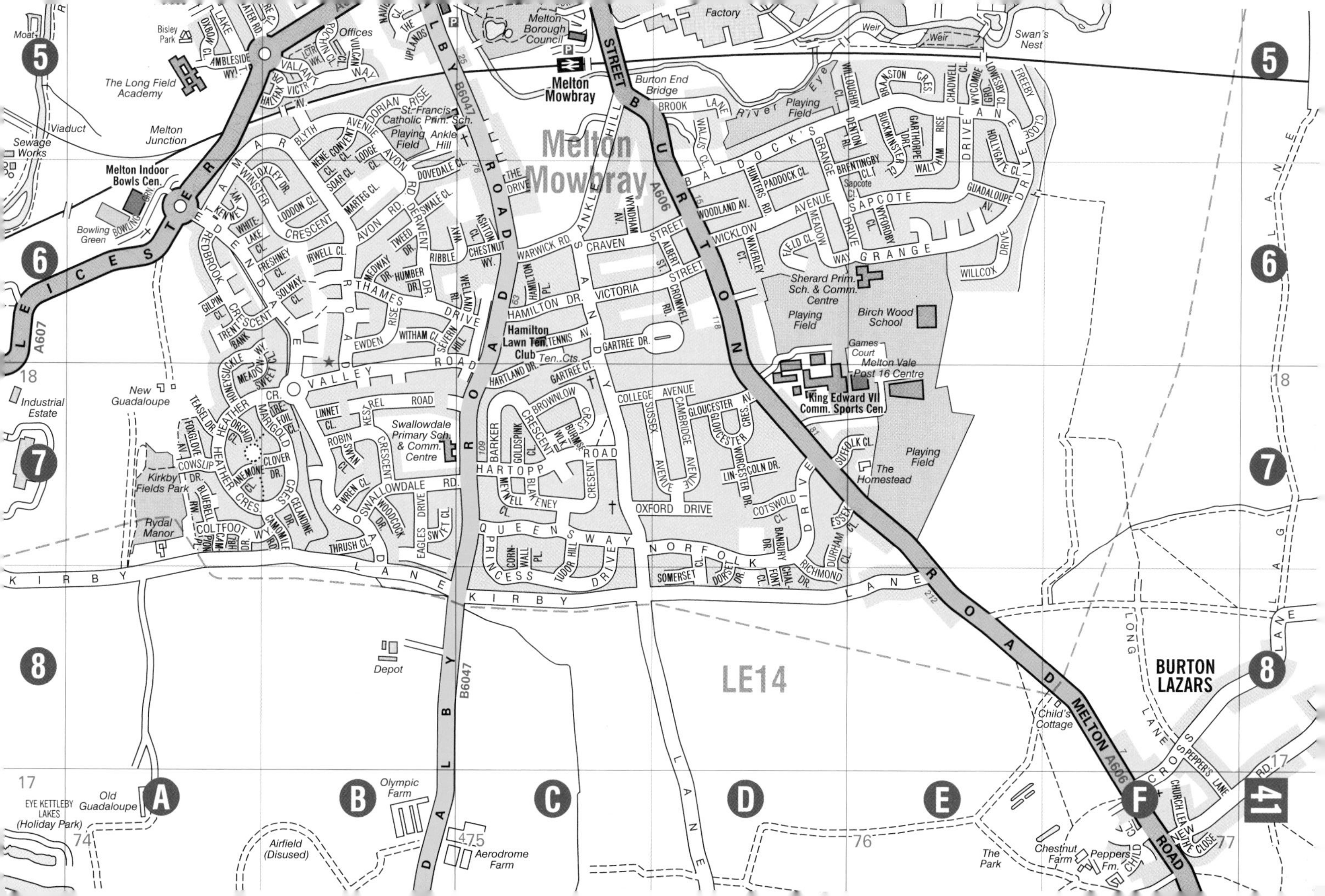

Melton Mowbray
BURTON LAZARS
LE14
Melton Borough Council
Melton Mowbray
Factory
Swan's Nest
Weir
Burton End Bridge
River Eye
Playing Field
The Long Field Academy
Bisley Park
Offices
Moat
Viaduct
Sewage Works
Melton Junction
Melton Indoor Bowls Cen.
Bowling Green
St. Francis Catholic Prim. Sch.
Ankle Hill
Sherard Prim. Sch. & Comm. Centre
Birch Wood School
Games Court
Melton Vale Post 16 Centre
King Edward VII Comm. Sports Cen.
The Homestead
Hamilton Lawn Ten. Club
Ten. Cts.
Swallowdale Primary Sch. & Comm. Centre
New Guadaloupe
Industrial Estate
Kirkby Fields Park
Rydal Manor
Depot
Olympic Farm
Aerodrome Farm
Airfield (Disused)
Old Guadaloupe
EYE KETTLEBY LAKES (Holiday Park)
Child's Cottage
The Park
Chestnut Farm
Peppers Fm.
LEICESTER ROAD
A607
DALBY ROAD
B6047
BURTON STREET
BURTON ROAD
MELTON ROAD
A606
KIRBY LANE
LONG LANE
CROSS LANE
PEPPER'S LANE
CHURCH LEA
NEW CLOSE
VALLEY ROAD
SAPCOTE DRIVE
GRANGE DRIVE
BALDOCK'S LANE
NORFOLK DRIVE
QUEENSWAY
PRINCESS DRIVE
A B C D E F
5 6 7 8
17 18 74 76 77

INDEX

Including Streets, Places & Areas, Hospitals etc., Industrial Estates,
Selected Flats & Walkways, Junction Names & Service Areas, Stations and Selected Places of Interest.

HOW TO USE THIS INDEX

1. Each street name is followed by its Postcode District, then by its Locality abbreviation(s) and then by its map reference;
e.g. **Alan Moss Rd.** LE11: Loug . . . .5D **14** is in the LE11 Postcode District and the Loughborough Locality and is to be found in square 5D on page **14**.
The page number is shown in bold type.

2. A strict alphabetical order is followed in which Av., Rd., St., etc. (though abbreviated) are read in full and as part of the street name;
e.g. **Brook La.** appears after **Brookland Way** but before **Brook Pk.**

3. Streets and a selection of flats and walkways that cannot be shown on the mapping, appear in the index with the thoroughfare to which they are
connected shown in brackets; e.g. **Arnold Smith Ho.** *LE12: Shep* . . . .5D **12** (off Bridge St.)

4. Addresses that are in more than one part are referred to as not continuous.

5. Places and areas are shown in the index in BLUE TYPE and the map reference is to the actual map square in which the town centre or area is located
and not to the place name shown on the map; e.g. BARROW UPON SOAR 4H 23

6. An example of a selected place of interest is Castle Donington Mus. 2F 5

7. Examples of stations are:
Barrow upon Soar Station (Rail) . . . .4H 23;   **Birstall (Park & Ride)** 6C 36

8. Junction names and Service Areas are shown in the index in **BOLD CAPITAL TYPE**; e.g. **DONINGTON PARK SERVICE AREA** 6B 6

9. An example of a Hospital, Hospice or selected Healthcare facility is LOUGHBOROUGH HOSPITAL 5E 15

GENERAL ABBREVIATIONS

Av. : Avenue	**Est.** : Estate	**Lit.** : Little	**Rd.** : Road
Blvd. : Boulevard	**Fld.** : Field	**Lwr.** : Lower	**Rdbt.** : Roundabout
Bri. : Bridge	**Flds.** : Fields	**Mnr.** : Manor	**Shop.** : Shopping
Bus. : Business	**Gdn.** : Garden	**Mkt.** : Market	**Sth.** : South
Cvn. : Caravan	**Gdns.** : Gardens	**Mdw.** : Meadow	**Sq.** : Square
Cen. : Centre	**Gth.** : Garth	**M.** : Mews	**St.** : Street
Cl. : Close	**Ga.** : Gate	**Mt.** : Mount	**Ter.** : Terrace
Comn. : Common	**Gt.** : Great	**Mus.** : Museum	**Trad.** : Trading
Cnr. : Corner	**Grn.** : Green	**Nth.** : North	**Up.** : Upper
Cotts. : Cottages	**Gro.** : Grove	**Pde.** : Parade	**Va.** : Vale
Ct. : Court	**Hgts.** : Heights	**Pk.** : Park	**Vw.** : View
Cres. : Crescent	**Ho.** : House	**Pas.** : Passage	**Vis.** : Visitors
Cft. : Croft	**Ind.** : Industrial	**Pl.** : Place	**Wlk.** : Walk
Dr. : Drive	**Info.** : Information	**Prom.** : Promenade	**W.** : West
E. : East	**La.** : Lane	**Ri.** : Rise	**Yd.** : Yard

LOCALITY ABBREVIATIONS

Anstey: LE7 . . . . .Anst	**East Goscote**: LE7 . . . . .E Gos	**Newtown Linford**: LE6 . . . . .New L	**Sutton Bonington**: DE74, LE12 . . .Sut B
Barkby: LE7 . . . . .Bark	**East Leake**: LE12 . . . . .East L	**Normanton on Soar**: LE12 . . . .Norm S	**Swithland**: LE12 . . . . .Swith
Barrow upon Soar: LE12 . . . .Bar S	**Hathern**: LE12 . . . . .Hath	**Nottingham East Midlands Airport**:	**Syston**: LE7 . . . . .Sys
Beaumont Leys: LE4 . . . . . .Beau L	**Hemington**: DE74 . . . . .Hem	DE74 . . . . .Nott A	**Thorpe Arnold**: LE14 . . . . .T Arn
Belton: DE74,LE12 . . . . .Belt	**Hoton**: LE12 . . . . .Hot	**Prestwold**: LE12 . . . . .Prestw	**Thrussington**: LE7 . . . . .Thru
Birstall: LE4 . . . . .Birs	**Isley Walton**: DE74 . . . . .I Wal	**Queniborough**: LE7 . . . . .Quen	**Thurcaston**: LE7 . . . . .Thurc
Brentingby: LE14 . . . . .Bren	**Kegworth**: DE74 . . . . .Keg	**Quorn**: LE12 . . . . .Quo	**Thurmaston**: LE4 . . . . .Thurm
Burton Lazars: LE14 . . . . .Bur L	**Kingston on Soar**: NG11 . . . . .King	**Ratcliffe on Soar**: NG11 . . . . . .Rat	**Ulverscroft**: LE67 . . . . .Ulv
Burton on the Wolds: LE12 . .Bur W	**Kirby Bellars**: LE14 . . . . . . .K Bel	**Ratcliffe on the Wreake**:	**Walton on the Wolds**: LE12 . . .Walt W
Castle Donington: DE74 . . . .C Don	**Leicester**: LE4 . . . . .Leic	LE7 . . . . .Rat W	**Wanlip**: LE4,LE7 . . . . .Wan
Charley: LE12,LE67 . . . . .Char	**Lockington**: DE74 . . . . .Lock	**Rearsby**: LE7 . . . . .Rear	**Welby**: LE14 . . . . .Welb
Coalville: LE12,LE67 . . . . .Coal	**Long Whatton**: LE12 . . . . . .Long W	**Rothley**: LE7 . . . . .R'ley	**Whitwick**: LE67 . . . . .Whit
Cossington: LE7,LE12 . . . . . . .Coss	**Loughborough**: LE11-12 . . . . .Loug	**Seagrave**: LE12 . . . . .Sea	**Woodhouse**: LE12 . . . . .Woodh
Cotes: LE12 . . . . .Cote	**Melton Mowbray**: LE13-14 . .Mel M	**Shepshed**: LE12 . . . . .Shep	**Woodhouse Eaves**: LE12 . . .Woodh E
Cropston: LE7 . . . . .Crop	**Mountsorrel**: LE12 . . . . .Moun	**Sileby**: LE12 . . . . .Sileby	**Woodthorpe**: LE12 . . . . .Wood
Diseworth: DE74 . . . . .Dise	**Nanpantan**: LE11-12 . . . . .Nan	**Stanford on Soar**: LE12 . . . .Stanf S	**Zouch**: LE12 . . . . .Zouch

A

	Albert Av. LE12: Sileby 1F **31**	**Ambassador Rd.** DE74: Nott A . . .5F **5**	**Archer Cl.** LE11: Loug 3B **14**
	Albert Pl. LE11: Loug 6H **15**	**Ambergate Dr.** LE4: Birs 6B **36**	**Archers Grn.** LE7: E Gos 6D **32**
Abberton Way LE11: Loug 1A **20**	**Albert Prom.** LE11: Loug 6A **16**	**Ambleside Cl.** LE11: Loug 3D **20**	**Arches, The** LE12: East L 2G **11**
Abbey Cl. LE12: Shep 2C **18**	**Albert St.** LE7: Sys 4B **38**	**Ambleside Way**	**Arden Dr.** LE13: Mel M 3A **40**
Abbey Rd. LE12: Char, Coal . . .5B **18**	LE11: Loug 6H **15**	LE13: Mel M 5A **41**	**Argonaut Av.** DE74: C Don 1D **4**
LE67: Char, Coal 6A **18**	LE13: Mel M 6D **41**	**Amis Cl.** LE11: Loug 4C **14**	**Argosy Rd.** DE74: Nott A 5H **5**
Abbotts Cl. LE7: Sys 4H **37**	**Albion Pde.** LE7: Sys 4B **38**	**Anchor Cl.** LE12: Hath 1A **14**	**Armitage Cl.** LE11: Loug 5G **15**
Abingdon Rd. LE13: Mel M 1A **40**	**Albion Rd.** LE12: Sileby 2E **31**	**Anchor La.** LE12: Hath 6A **10**	**Armitage Dr.** LE7: R'ley 2B **36**
Acacia Av. LE4: Birs 6D **36**	**Albion St.** LE7: Sys 4B **38**	**Anemone Cl.** LE13: Mel M 7A **41**	**Armston Rd.** LE12: Quo 6E **23**
Acer Cl. LE11: Loug 4G **21**	**Alder Rd.** LE12: Bar S 2G **23**	**Angel Yd.** LE11: Loug 5H **15**	**Arnold Smith Ho.**
Acres Ri. LE13: Mel M 3E **40**	**Alexander Rd.** LE12: Quo 4D **22**	**Angrave Cl.** LE12: East L 1G **11**	*LE12: Shep* 5D **12**
Adam Dale LE11: Loug 6F **15**	**Alfred St.** LE11: Loug 4H **15**	**Angus Dr.** LE11: Loug 5D **14**	*(off Bridge St.)*
Adcock Cl. LE13: Mel M 2F **40**	**Algernon Rd.** LE13: Mel M 4D **40**	**Ankle Hill** LE13: Mel M 6C **41**	**Arthur St.** LE11: Loug 6G **15**
Adcocks Cl. LE11: Loug 4H **15**	**Allen Av.** LE12: Quo 4D **22**	**Annies Wharf** LE11: Loug 4H **15**	**Arundel Av.** DE74: C Don 1C **4**
Adkins Ct. LE12: Bar S 3G **23**	**Allendale Rd.** LE11: Loug 4H **15**	**Anson Rd.** DE74: Nott A 5E **5**	**Arundel Cl.** LE12: Moun 5G **29**
Aerodrome Cl. LE11: Loug 2E **15**	**Allington Dr.** LE4: Birs 6D **36**	LE12: Shep 6B **12**	**Arundel Gro.** LE12: Shep 1C **18**
Afton Cl. LE11: Loug 6B **14**	**All Saints Rd.** LE7: Thurc 5F **35**	**Anstey La.** LE7: Thurc 6E **35**	**Asfordby Rd.** LE13: Mel M 4A **40**
Aingarth LE11: Loug 6A **16**	**All Saints Vw.** LE11: Loug 4H **15**	**Anthony Cl.** LE7: Sys 5G **37**	**Ashby Cres.** LE11: Loug 6D **14**
Ainsworth Dr. LE12: Sileby 1G **31**	**Allsopp's La.** LE11: Loug 5G **21**	**Anthony St.** LE7: R'ley 1A **36**	**Ashby Gro.** LE11: Loug 5E **15**
Aitken Way LE11: Loug 5G **21**	**Almond Cl.** LE11: Loug 5G **21**	**Apiary Ga.** DE74: C Don 2F **5**	**Ashby Rd.** DE74: Keg 6B **6**
Alan Moss Rd. LE11: Loug 5D **14**	**Alston Dr.** LE11: Loug 3D **14**	**Apple Tree Way** LE12: Bar S . . .2H **23**	LE11: Loug 5E **15**
Alan Turing Rd. LE11: Loug . . .5H **21**	**Althorpe Dr.** LE11: Loug 4C **14**	**Arbury Dale** LE12: Shep 1E **19**	LE12: Long W 1B **12**
Albany St. LE11: Loug 4E **15**	**Alvaston Rd.** LE13: Mel M 2A **40**	**Archdale Cl.** LE4: Birs 6C **36**	**Ashby Rd. Central**
	Alvis Dale LE7: R'ley 5B **30**	**Archdale St.** LE7: Sys 4H **37**	LE12: Shep 2D **18**

Ashby Rd. E. LE12: Shep 2E **19**
Ashby Rd. W.
LE12: Belt, Shep 2A **18**
Ashby Sq. LE11: Loug 5G **15**
Ash Cl. LE12: Bar S 2H **23**
Ashdown Cl. LE11: Loug 4C **14**
Ash Dr. LE7: Sys 5B **38**
Ash Gro. LE12: Hath 5A **10**
LE12: Moun 4A **30**
LE13: Mel M 2B **40**
Ashleigh Dr. LE11: Loug 1E **21**
Ashmead Cres. LE4: Birs 6E **37**
Ashton Cl. LE13: Mel M 6C **41**
Ash Wlk. LE12: East L 4F **11**
Aspen Av. LE11: Loug 4G **21**
Atherstone Rd. LE11: Loug 4F **21**
Atterbury Cl. LE12: Bar S 4H **23**
Augustus Cl. LE7: Sys 5H **37**
Aumberry Gap LE11: Loug 5H **15**
Auster Cres. LE7: Rear 4F **33**
Avenue Cl. LE7: Quen 2D **38**
Avenue Rd. LE7: Quen 2E **39**
LE12: Sileby 2F **31**
Avery Dr. LE7: Sys 2B **38**
Avon Rd. LE12: Bar S 5H **23**
LE13: Mel M 5B **41**
Avon Va. Rd. LE11: Loug 2A **22**
Ayces Cotts. LE13: Mel M 4A **40**

B

Babington Ct. LE7: R'ley 1A **36**
Babington Rd. LE7: R'ley 1A **36**
LE12: Bar S 3H **23**
Back La. DE74: C Don 1E **5**
LE7: Coss 6F **31**
LE7: Thru 1F **33**
LE12: Cote 3D **16**
LE12: Sileby 2E **31**
Badger Ct. LE11: Loug 3D **20**
Badgers Bank LE7: R'ley 6A **30**
Badger's Cnr. LE7: E Gos 5D **32**
Badgers Wlk. LE12: Quo 6C **22**
Badminton Rd. LE7: Sys 2B **38**
Bagley Cl. LE11: Loug 3C **14**
Bailey Cl. LE11: Loug 3D **20**
Bainbridge Rd. LE11: Loug 2A **22**
Bakewell Dr. DE74: C Don 3E **5**
Bakewell Rd. LE11: Loug 2E **15**
Baldock's La. LE13: Mel M 6D **41**
Balliol Av. LE7: Sys 5C **38**
Balmoral Av. LE12: Shep 1C **18**
Balmoral Rd. LE12: Moun 4H **29**
LE13: Mel M 2C **40**
Bampton St. LE11: Loug 6H **15**
Banbury Dr. LE12: Shep 6B **12**
LE13: Mel M 7D **41**
Bandalls La. LE12: Bar S 4E **17**
Banks, The LE7: Quen 2E **39**
LE12: Bar S 3H **23**
LE12: Sea 3H **25**
LE12: Sileby 2E **31**
Banks Cl. LE12: Sileby 2E **31**
Barden Cl. LE11: Loug 6B **14**
BARKBY 6C **38**
Barkby La. LE7: Sys 5H **37**
Barkby Rd. LE7: Quen 4E **39**
LE7: Sys 3B **38**
Barkby Thorpe La.
LE4: Thurm 6G **37**
Barker Cres. LE13: Mel M 7C **41**
Barley Way LE7: R'ley 6A **30**
Barnards Dr. LE12: Sileby 1G **31**
Barnard Way LE12: Moun 4H **29**
Barn Cl. DE74: C Don 2F **5**
Barnett Cl. LE7: Coss 6F **31**
Barnfield Cl. LE12: Long W 3D **8**
Barngate Cl. LE13: Mel M 2D **40**
Barn Mdw. Rd. LE4: Wan 6B **36**
Barnsdale Cl. LE11: Loug 4G **15**
Barons Ct. LE12: Moun 2A **30**
Barons Way LE12: Moun 2A **30**
Barrack Row LE11: Loug 4H **15**
Barradale Av. LE12: Sileby 1E **31**
Barrett Dr. LE11: Loug 3D **14**
Barrington Ct. LE12: Sut B 1B **10**
Barroon DE74: C Don 2F **5**
Barrowcliffe Cl. LE12: Bar S . . .3G **23**
Barrow Rd. LE12: Bur W 6G **17**
LE12: Cote 3D **16**
LE12: Quo 5D **22**
LE12: Sileby 6C **24**
Barrow Rd. Bus. Pk.
LE12: Sileby 2E **31**
Barrow St. LE11: Loug 6H **15**
BARROW UPON SOAR 4H **23**
Barrow upon Soar Station (Rail)
. . . . .4H **23**
Barr Rd. LE7: Sys 5A **38**
Barry Dr. LE7: Sys 3B **38**
Barsby Dr. LE11: Loug 3D **14**
Bartholomew Cl. LE7: R'ley 1C **36**
Bateman Rd. LE12: East L 3F **11**
Bates Cl. LE11: Loug 3B **14**
Bates Hollow Dr. LE7: R'ley 2B **36**
Bath St. LE7: Sys 3A **38**
Baxter Ga. LE11: Loug 5H **15**
Bayliss Cl. LE12: Quo 4D **22**
Bayswater Rd. LE13: Mel M . . .3D **40**
Beacon Av. LE11: Loug 2F **21**
LE12: Quo 6C **22**
Beacon Dr. LE11: Loug 2G **21**
Beacon Hill Country Pk. 3D **26**
Beacon Rd. LE11: Loug 3F **21**
LE12: Woodh E 4B **26**
Beaconsfield Rd.
LE13: Mel M 2A **40**
Beardsley Rd. LE12: Quo 5D **22**
Beatty Rd. LE7: Sys 3B **38**
Beaufort Av. LE11: Loug 3G **21**
Beaumanor Dr.
LE12: Woodh 1A **28**
Beaumanor Gdns.
LE12: Woodh 1A **28**
Beaumaris Cres.
LE12: Shep 1C **18**
Beaumaris Rd. LE12: Moun . . .5G **29**
Beaumont Ct. LE11: Loug 3G **15**
Beaumont Gdns.
LE13: Mel M 2C **40**
Beaumont Rd. LE11: Loug 3H **21**
LE12: Bar S 3G **23**
Beck Cres. LE11: Loug 5F **21**
Beckmill Apartments
LE13: Mel M 4D **40**
Beckmill Ct. LE13: Mel M 4D **40**
Beckmill La. LE13: Mel M 4D **40**
Becks Cl. LE4: Birs 6B **36**
Bedford Cl. DE74: Keg 4F **7**
Bedford Sq. LE11: Loug 6H **15**
Bedford St. LE11: Loug 6H **15**
Beeby Cl. LE7: Sys 4C **38**
Beech Av. LE12: East L 4F **11**
Beech Cl. LE12: Shep 5E **13**
Beech Dr. LE7: Sys 5B **38**
Beeches Av. LE12: Moun 3A **30**
Beeches Rd. LE11: Loug 1A **22**
Beechwood Av. LE7: Quen 2D **38**
LE13: Mel M 2E **40**
Beedles Lake Golf Course 5C **32**
Bee Hive La. LE11: Loug 6H **15**
Belfry Pl. LE12: Shep 3C **18**
Bell Centre, The
LE13: Mel M 4C **40**
Belmont Way LE11: Loug 1A **20**
Belton Pk. LE11: Loug 3G **15**
Belton Rd. LE11: Loug 4F **15**
Belton Rd. W. LE11: Loug 3E **15**
Belton Rd. W. Extension
LE11: Loug 3F **15**
Belton's Cotts. LE12: East L . . .1G **11**
Belton St. LE12: Shep 5D **12**
Belvoir Cl. LE12: Moun 5H **29**
Belvoir Dr. LE7: Sys 3C **38**
LE11: Loug 3F **21**
Belvoir St. LE13: Mel M 3E **40**
Belvoir Way LE12: Shep 1C **18**
Bennet Dr. LE13: Mel M 1C **40**
Bennett's La. LE7: Coss 5F **31**
Benscliffe Dr. LE11: Loug 1E **21**
Benscliffe Rd. LE6: New L 6C **26**
LE67: Ulv 6C **26**
Bentley Cl. LE11: Loug 6A **16**
Bentley Rd. DE74: C Don 1D **4**
Bentley St. LE13: Mel M 4C **40**
Beresford Ct. LE12: Shep 5E **13**
Berkeley Cl. LE12: Moun 4A **30**
Berkeley Cl. Pk. Homes
LE12: Moun 4A **30**
Berkeley Rd. LE11: Loug 3C **20**
Berrycott La. LE12: Sea 3H **25**
Betty Henser's La.
LE12: Moun 1H **29**
Bevan Rd. LE4: Leic 6G **35**
Beveridge St. LE12: Bar S 4H **23**
Beverley Rd. DE74: Nott A 5H **5**
Bickley Av. LE13: Mel M 3D **40**
Biggin, The DE74: C Don 2F **5**
Biggin St. LE11: Loug 5H **15**
Big La. LE12: Bar S, Sea 1E **25**
Birch Av. LE12: Bar S 2H **23**
Birch Cl. LE11: Loug 5G **21**
LE13: Mel M 2B **40**
Birches, The DE74: Dise 6G **5**
Birch Lea LE12: East L 3F **11**
Birchtree Av. LE4: Birs 6C **36**
Birchwood Cl. LE7: Sys 4C **38**
BIRD HILL 4F **27**
Bird Hill Rd. LE12: Woodh E . . .3F **27**
Birstall Local Nature Reserve
. . . . .6E **37**
Birstall Mdw. LE4: Birs, Wan . . .6A **36**
Birstall (Park & Ride) 6C **36**
Bishop Mdw. Rd.
LE11: Loug 1E **15**
Bishop's Meadow Local Nature
Reserve 1F **15**
Bishop St. LE11: Loug 5A **16**
LE13: Mel M 4D **40**
Bisley Pk. LE13: Mel M 5A **41**
Blackberry La. LE7: Coss 5G **31**
Blackbird Cl. LE12: East L 1H **11**
Blackbrook Cl. LE12: Shep 6C **12**
Blackbrook Ct. LE11: Loug 3E **15**
Blackbrook Rd. LE11: Loug 6C **14**
Blackbrook Way LE11: Loug 4B **14**
Blackfriars Rd. LE7: Sys 5D **38**
Blackham Rd. LE11: Loug 2G **21**
Black La. LE12: Walt W 1D **24**
Blacksmiths Av. LE12: Shep . . .4E **13**
Blacksmiths Cl. LE7: Thru 1F **33**
Blackthorn Dr. LE7: Sys 4H **37**
Blair Cl. LE12: Moun 5G **29**
Blake Cl. LE12: Bar S 2G **23**
Blake Dr. LE11: Loug 4D **14**
Blakeney Cres. LE13: Mel M . . .7C **41**
Bleakmoor Cl. LE7: Rear 2G **33**
Blenheim Cl. LE11: Loug 5C **14**
Blenheim Rd. LE4: Birs 6D **36**
Blenheim Wlk. LE13: Mel M 2B **40**
Bley Av. LE12: East L 4F **11**
Blithfield Av. LE11: Loug 6C **14**
Bluebell Cl. LE7: Quen 1E **39**
Bluebell Dr. LE11: Loug 2F **21**
Bluebell Row LE13: Mel M 7A **41**
Blue Granite Pk.
LE12: Moun 3A **30**
Blyth Av. LE13: Mel M 5B **41**
Blyth Ct. DE74: C Don 1F **5**
Bond Cl. LE11: Loug 2A **22**
Bondgate DE74: C Don 2F **5**
Bond La. LE12: Moun 3G **29**
Booth End LE11: Loug 3B **14**
Borough St. DE74: C Don 2F **5**
DE74: Keg 3F **7**
Borrowdale Way LE11: Loug . . .2D **20**
Borrowell DE74: Keg 2E **7**
Bosworth Rd. DE74: C Don 2D **4**
Bottleacre La. LE11: Loug 2G **15**
(not continuous)
Boundary Rd. LE12: Moun 4H **29**
Boundary Way LE12: Shep 4E **13**
Bowler Ct. LE11: Loug 5A **16**
Bowler Way LE11: Loug 5E **15**
Bowley, The DE74: Dise 6A **8**
Bowley Av. LE13: Mel M 2E **40**
Bowley Ct. LE13: Mel M 4C **40**
Bowling Grn. LE13: Mel M 6A **41**
Bowling Grn. Cl.
LE12: Sileby 1F **31**
Boyer St. LE11: Loug 5A **16**
Boyle Dr. LE11: Loug 5H **21**
Bracken Dale LE7: E Gos 6E **33**
Brackenfield Way
LE4: Thurm 6A **38**
Braddon Rd. LE11: Loug 3C **14**
Bradgate Cl. LE12: Moun 1H **29**
LE12: Sileby 2E **31**
Bradgate Country Pk. 5A **34**
Bradgate Country Pk. Vis. Cen.
. . . . .6A **34**
Bradgate Rd. LE7: Crop 4B **34**
LE11: Loug 3E **21**
Braemar Cl. LE12: Moun 5H **29**
Bramble Cl. LE11: Loug 4E **15**
Bramcote Rd. LE11: Loug 4F **21**
Bramley Cl. LE12: Sileby 1F **31**
LE13: Mel M 2B **40**
Bramley Ct. LE12: East L 3G **11**
Brampton Rd. LE13: Mel M 1A **40**
Brand Hill LE12: Woodh E 5G **27**
Brand La.
LE12: Woodh, Woodh E . . .3H **27**
Branston Av. LE12: Bar S 3A **24**
Branston Cres. LE13: Mel M . . .5E **41**
Breachfield Rd. LE12: Bar S . . .4H **23**
Breadcroft La. LE12: Bar S 3H **23**
Breakback Rd.
LE12: Woodh E 2D **26**
Breech Hedge LE7: R'ley 6A **30**
Brendon Cl. LE12: Shep 2E **19**
Brentingby Cl. LE13: Mel M . . .6D **41**
Breward Way LE13: Mel M 1D **40**
Brians Cl. LE7: Sys 3C **38**
Briargate Dr. LE4: Birs 6A **36**
Brickcliffe Rd. LE12: East L 2H **11**
Brick Kiln La. LE12: Shep 2C **18**
Brickley Cres. LE12: East L 3H **11**
Brickwood Pl. LE12: Bur W 5G **17**
Bridge Cl. LE4: Thurm 6H **37**
Bridge Flds. DE74: Keg 2G **7**
Bridge Grn. LE4: Birs 6B **36**
Bridgeland Rd. LE11: Loug 5A **16**
Bridgeside Cotts.
LE11: Loug 4G **15**
Bridge St. LE11: Loug 5G **15**
LE12: Bar S 4G **23**
LE12: Shep 5D **12**
Bridle Cl. LE13: Mel M 2A **40**
Brighton Av. LE7: Sys 3C **38**
Brightside Av. LE13: Mel M 3A **40**
Brinks, The LE12: Quo 6F **23**
Brisco Av. LE11: Loug 3F **15**
Briscoe La. LE12: Woodh 1H **27**
Bristlecone Cl. LE12: Bar S 2G **23**
Britannia St. LE12: Shep 5D **12**
Britannia Way LE4: Thurm 6G **37**
Britannia Works LE4: Thurm . . .6G **37**
British School Gdns.
LE13: Mel M 4C ***40***
(off Chapel St.)
BROAD HILL 3G **29**
Broadhill Rd. DE74: Keg 3E **7**
Broad St. LE7: Sys 4A **38**
LE11: Loug 5G **15**
Broadway LE7: Sys 4A **38**
LE11: Loug 3G **21**
Brockington Pl. LE11: Loug 6F **15**
Brockington Rd.
LE13: Mel M 1C **40**
Brocklehurst Rd.
LE13: Mel M 2E **40**
Brokesby Dr. LE4: Birs 6B **36**
Bromhead St. LE11: Loug 4A **16**
Brook End LE12: East L 2G **11**
Brooker Cl. LE12: Bar S 2G **23**
Brookfield Av. LE7: Sys 4B **38**
LE11: Loug 2E **21**
Brookfield Ct. LE13: Mel M 2B **40**
Brookfield Rd. LE7: R'ley 2A **36**
Brookfield St. LE7: Sys 4B **38**
LE13: Mel M 2B **40**
Brookfields Way
LE12: East L 2G **11**
Brook Furlong Dr. *LE4: Birs 6B* ***36***
(off Hallam Flds. Rd.)
Brookhouse Cl. LE7: Rear 4G **33**
Brookland Way LE12: Moun . . .5A **30**
Brook La. LE11: Loug 3D **20**
LE12: Bar S 3H **23**
LE13: Mel M 5D **41**
Brook Pk. LE7: Rear 4G **33**
Brook Rd. LE12: Woodh E 1D **26**
Brook Side LE11: Loug 5G **15**
Brookside DE74: Dise 6A **8**
LE7: Rear 3G **33**
LE7: Sys 3A **38**
(not continuous)
LE12: East L 4G **11**
Brookside Av. LE12: East L 3F **11**
Brookside Cl. LE12: Bar S 2H **23**
LE12: Shep 1E **19**
Brookside Rd. LE11: Loug 3D **20**
Brook St. LE7: Rear 4G **33**
LE7: Sys 3A **38**
LE12: Bur W 5G **17**
LE12: Shep 5D **12**
LE12: Sileby 2E **31**
LE13: Mel M 4D **40**
Broom Av. LE11: Loug 4G **21**
Broombriggs Farm
& Windmill Hill Country Pk.
. . . . .4E **27**
Broome Av. LE7: E Gos 5E **33**
Broome La.
LE7: E Gos, Rat W 4B **32**
Broomfield LE7: E Gos 6E **33**
Broughton Cl. LE11: Loug 5C **14**
Brown Av. LE12: Quo 5E **23**

Brownhill Cres.—Cromwell Rd.

Brownhill Cres. LE7: R'ley 2F 35
Browning Cl. LE13: Mel M 1C 40
Browning Rd. LE11: Loug 5D 14
Brownlow Cres.
LE13: Mel M 7C 41
Browns La. LE11: Loug 6G 15
Brunsleigh Cft. LE12: Hath 1A 14
Brush Dr. LE11: Loug 3H 15
Brushfield Av. LE12: Sileby 1F 31
Bruxby St. LE7: Sys 4H 37
Bryan Cl. LE12: Bar S 3H 23
Buckhorn Sq. LE11: Loug 5A 16
Buckingham Dr. LE11: Loug 4C 14
Buckminster Cl.
LE13: Mel M 5E 41
Buckthron Dr. LE12: Bar S 2G 23
Buddon Ct. LE12: Moun 4A 30
Buddon La. LE12: Quo 1C 28
Bull Ring LE12: Shep 6D 12
Bulrush Cl. LE12: Moun 4B 30
Bulstrode Pl. DE74: Keg 3E 7
BUNKER HILL 5F 13
Burbage Cl. LE11: Loug 3E 15
Burder St. LE11: Loug 3A 16
Burfield Av. LE11: Loug 6G 15
Burleigh Rd. LE11: Loug 5G 15
Burley Ri. DE74: Keg 4F 7
Burmese Wlk. LE13: Mel M 7C 41
Burnaston Way LE11: Loug 4A 22
Burns Cl. LE13: Mel M 1B 40
Burns Rd. LE11: Loug 4D 14
Burrow Dr. LE7: R'ley 2B 36
Burrows, The LE7: E Gos 6C 32
LE12: East L 2G 11
BURTON BANDALLS 4E 17
Burton Hall LE12: Bur W 6G 17
Burton La. LE12: Bur W 3F 17
BURTON LAZARS 8F 41
BURTON ON THE WOLDS 5H 17
Burton Rd. LE12: Sileby 2E 31
LE13: Mel M 5C 41
Burtons Rd. LE7: R'ley 2B 36
Burton St. LE11: Loug 1H 21
LE13: Mel M 4C 40
Burton Wlk. LE12: East L 3G 11
LE12: Sileby 1E 31
Burton Walks LE11: Loug 1H 21
Butcher's La. LE12: Sea 3H 25
Butler Way LE12: Sileby 3F 31
Buttercup Cl. LE12: Moun 3B 30
Buttercup La. LE12: Shep 6B 12
Buttercup Rd. LE11: Loug 5G 21
Butterley Dr. LE11: Loug 1B 20
Buttermere Cl. LE13: Mel M 5A 41
Buttermere Way LE12: Bar S 2G 23
Butthole La. LE11: Loug 5E 13
LE12: Shep 5E 13
Butt La. LE12: Norm S 4D 10
Byland Way LE11: Loug 4B 14
Byron St. LE11: Loug 4E 15
Byron St. Extension
LE11: Loug 4E 15
Byron Way LE13: Mel M 2B 40

C

Cabin Leas LE11: Loug 3H 15
Caernarvon Cl. LE12: Moun 5H 29
LE12: Shep 1C 18
Caincross Cl. LE11: Loug 4H 21
Caldwell St. LE11: Loug 5G 15
Calke Cl. LE11: Loug 5G 21
Caloe Cl. LE12: Sileby 2G 31
Cambridge Av. LE13: Mel M 7D 41
Cambridge Cl. LE7: Sys 4C 38
Cambridge St. LE11: Loug 4H 15
LE12: Shep 1D 18
Camomile Rd. LE13: Mel M 7B 41
Campion Hill DE74: C Don 1E 5
Campion Pl. LE13: Mel M 7A 41
Canal Bank LE11: Loug 4G 15
Canalbridge Cl. LE11: Loug 5B 16
Canning Way LE11: Loug 3C 14
Canterbury Dr. LE13: Mel M 1A 40
Carillon Ct. LE11: Loug 5H 15
Carington St. LE11: Loug 4F 15
Carisbrooke Rd.
LE12: Moun 5G 29
Carlton Cl. LE11: Loug 4F 15
Carlton Cres. LE12: East L 2H 11
Carnegie Cres. LE13: Mel M 1E 40
Carnival Way DE74: C Don 1F 5
CARR HILL 5C 12
Carr La. LE12: Shep 4A 12
Carrs Cl. DE74: C Don 2E 5
Cartland Dr. LE11: Loug 3C 14
Cartwright St. LE11: Loug 4H 15
Carver's Path LE7: E Gos 6E 33
Castledine Av. LE12: Quo 4E 23
Castledine St. LE11: Loug 1H 21
LE12: Quo 5D 22
Castledine St. Extension
LE11: Loug 1H 21
CASTLE DONINGTON 2F 5
Castle Donington Community College Leisure Cen. 2F 5
Castle Donington Mus. 2F 5
Castle Hill DE74: C Don 1F 5
LE12: East L 4H 11
LE12: Moun 3A 30
(not continuous)
Castle Rd. LE12: Moun 4H 29
Catherines Cl. LE12: Quo 5F 23
Cattle Mkt. LE11: Loug 6H 15
Cauby Cl. LE12: Sileby 2G 31
Caudle Cl. LE7: Crop 4D 34
Causeway LE12: Quo 4G 23
Causeway La. LE7: Crop 5C 34
Cavalry Cl. LE13: Mel M 1A 40
Cavendish Cl. DE74: C Don 3E 5
Cave Rd. LE12: Bar S 3H 23
Cawdell Dr. LE12: Long W 5F 9
Caxton Pl. LE12: Bar S 4H 23
Cedar Av. LE12: East L 4F 11
Cedar Dr. LE7: Sys 5B 38
LE13: Mel M 2B 40
Cedar Gro. LE12: Moun 4A 30
Cedar Rd. DE74: C Don 3F 5
LE11: Loug 2A 22
Celandine Cl. LE12: Moun 3B 30
Celandine Dr. LE13: Mel M 7B 41
Celandine Rd. LE12: Shep 6B 12
Cemetery Rd. LE12: Sileby 2F 31
Central Av. LE7: Sys 3B 38
LE12: Shep 6D 12
Cessna Ct. DE74: C Don 2D 4
Chadwell Cl. LE13: Mel M 5E 41
Chainbridge Cl. LE11: Loug 4G 15
Chalfont Cl. LE13: Mel M 8D 41
Chalfont Dr. LE12: Sileby 4E 31
Challottee LE12: Shep 6E 13
Chalmondley Dr.
LE13: Mel M 1D 40
Chamberlains Fld. LE4: Birs 6B 36
Chantry Cl. LE12: Quo 5E 23
Chapel Cl. LE7: Sys 3B 38
LE7: Thurc 4F 35
Chapel Ct. LE12: Shep 4D 12
Chapel La. LE12: Bur W 5H 17
Chapel St. LE7: Sys 3A 38
LE12: Shep 4D 12
LE13: Mel M 4C 40
Chaplin Cl. LE12: Sileby 2E 31
Chapman St. LE11: Loug 5A 16
Charles Hall Cl. LE12: Shep 5E 13
Charles St. LE11: Loug 4H 15
LE12: Sileby 3E 31
Charley Dr. LE11: Loug 1E 21
Charley Rd.
LE12: Shep, Char, Nan, Woodh E 3A 26
Charlotte St. LE13: Mel M 4C 40
Charnia Gro. LE12: Swith 1D 34
Charnwood Av. DE74: C Don 2G 5
LE12: Sut B 2C 10
Charnwood Dr. LE13: Mel M 3A 40
Charnwood Edge Bus. Pk.
LE7: Coss 6H 31
Charnwood Flds.
LE12: Sut B 2C 10
Charnwood Forester End
LE11: Loug 4F 15
Charnwood Golf Cen. 2C 14
Charnwood Mus. 6G 15
Charnwood Ri.
LE12: Woodh E 5F 27
Charnwood Rd. LE11: Loug 1H 21
LE12: Shep 2D 18
Charteris Cl. LE11: Loug 3D 14
Chase, The LE7: E Gos 5D 32
Chatsworth Cl. LE12: Shep 6C 12
Chatsworth Dr. LE7: Sys 4H 37
Chatsworth Rd. LE11: Loug 4D 14
Chaveney Ct. LE12: Quo 6C 22
Chaveney Rd. LE12: Quo 6C 22
Chaveney Wlk. LE12: Quo 6C 22
Cheapside LE13: Mel M 4C 40
Checkland Rd. LE4: Thurm 6H 37
Chelker Way LE11: Loug 6C 14
Cheribough Rd. DE74: C Don 2E 5
Cherry Cl. LE11: Loug 4G 21
Cherry Dr. LE7: Sys 5B 38
Cherwell Rd. LE12: Bar S 4H 23
Chester Cl. LE11: Loug 6F 15
Chestnut Cl. LE7: Quen 2D 38
LE7: Sys 5B 38
LE12: Quo 1C 28
LE12: Shep 6E 13
Chestnut Ct. LE12: Moun 3A 30
Chestnut Pl. LE12: Bar S 4H 23
Chestnuts Cl. LE12: Sut B 3H 7
Chestnut St. LE11: Loug 5G 15
Chestnut Way LE7: E Gos 6E 33
LE13: Mel M 6C 41
Chetwynd Dr. LE13: Mel M 4A 40
Cheviot Dr. LE12: Shep 6E 13
Chichester Cl. LE11: Loug 3C 20
Child Cl. LE14: Bur L 8F 41
Chiltern Av. LE12: Shep 6F 13
Chiswick Dr. LE11: Loug 5C 14
Christie Dr. LE11: Loug 3D 14
Church Cl. LE7: Sys 3B 38
LE12: East L 3G 11
Church Ga. DE74: Keg 3F 7
LE11: Loug 5H 15
LE12: Shep 5E 13
Church Ga. M. *LE11: Loug 5H 15*
(off Church Gate)
Church Hill LE12: Woodh E 4G 27
Church Hill Rd. LE12: Moun 4H 29
Churchill Cl. LE13: Mel M 2C 40
Church Lands LE11: Loug 3H 15
Church La. DE74: C Don 2F 5
DE74: Hem, Lock 1H 5
DE74: Lock 1B 6
LE7: Rat W 3C 32
LE7: Rear 3G 33
LE7: Thru 1F 33
LE12: Bar S 3H 23
LE12: Quo 5D 22
Church Lea LE14: Bur L 8F 41
Church Leys Av. LE7: Rear 3G 33
Church Rd. LE7: Wan 5E 37
Church Side LE12: Shep 5E 13
Church St. DE74: Lock 1B 6
LE7: R'ley 1B 36
LE12: Bar S 3H 23
LE12: Hath 6A 10
LE12: Sea 3H 25
LE12: Shep 5D 12
LE13: Mel M 4C 40
Church Ter. LE13: Mel M 5C 41
Citrus Gro. DE74: Keg 2E 7
City Hgts. LE11: Loug 5H 15
Claire Ct. LE12: Sileby 2G 31
Clapgun St. DE74: C Don 2F 5
Clarence St. LE11: Loug 4H 15
Clark Dr. LE13: Mel M 1C 40
Clarke Sq. LE7: R'ley 4B 30
Clawson Cl. LE11: Loug 3D 14
Cleeve Mt. LE11: Loug 5C 14
Clements Ga. DE74: Dise 5A 8
Cleveland Rd. LE11: Loug 4F 21
Cleves Cl. LE13: Mel M 4A 40
Cliff Av. LE11: Loug 4F 15
Clifford Rd. LE11: Loug 4F 15
Close, The LE14: Bur L 8F 41
Cloud Lea LE12: Moun 5A 30
Cloud Way Ct. LE11: Loug 3G 15
Clover Dr. LE13: Mel M 7B 41
Clover La. LE12: Moun 4B 30
Clover Wlk. LE7: E Gos 6E 33
Clover Way LE7: Sys 5A 38
Clowbridge Dr. LE11: Loug 6C 14
Clumber Cl. LE7: Sys 2B 38
LE11: Loug 5G 21
Clumber St. LE13: Mel M 3B 40
Clydesdale Cl. LE13: Mel M 1A 40
Coach Ho. Ct. *LE11: Loug 6H 15*
(off Woodgate)
Coachmans Ct. LE12: Shep 4E 13
Coach Rd. LE12: Shep 6E 13
(not continuous)
Coal Cart Rd. LE4: Wan 5B 36
Cobble Cl. LE12: Bar S 2H 23
Cobden St. LE11: Loug 5A 16
(not continuous)
Coe Av. LE11: Loug 4B 14
Colgrove Rd. LE11: Loug 1G 21
College Av. LE13: Mel M 7C 41
College Rd. LE7: Sys 5B 38
Colling Cl. LE11: Loug 3B 14
Collingwood Cl.
LE13: Mel M 4A 40
Collingwood Cres.
LE13: Mel M 4A 4
Collingwood Dr.
LE12: Sileby 1F 3
Coltfoot Way LE13: Mel M 7A 4
Compton Cl. LE11: Loug 3C 2
Condon Rd. LE12: Bar S 4A 24
Coneries, The LE11: Loug 5H 15
Conery La. LE12: Sea 2H 25
(not continuous)
Coniston Cres. LE11: Loug 2D 20
Coniston Rd. LE12: Bar S 3H 23
LE13: Mel M 1A 40
Connaught Ho. LE11: Loug 6H 15
Connery Leys Rd. LE4: Birs 6B 36
Convent Cl. LE13: Mel M 5B 41
Conway Cl. LE11: Loug 4C 14
Conway Dr. LE12: Shep 1B 18
LE13: Mel M 2C 40
Conway Rd. LE12: Moun 4H 29
Cooks Dr. DE74: C Don 2E 5
Cookson Pl. LE11: Loug 3C 14
Coombe Cl. LE12: Shep 1E 19
Cooper Ct. LE11: Loug 1B 22
Cooper's Nook LE7: E Gos 6D 32
Copeland Cres. LE11: Loug 4D 14
Copley Cl. LE13: Mel M 3E 40
Coplow Cres. LE7: Sys 5A 38
Coppice, The LE12: Quo 1F 29
Coppice La. LE7: Quen 2F 39
Copse Gro. LE11: Loug 5G 21
Copt Oak Rd. LE12: Nan 6G 19
Cordelia Dr. LE4: Birs 6B 36
Cordell Rd. LE11: Loug 3D 14
Cordwell Cl. DE74: C Don 1D 4
Cornwall Pl. LE13: Mel M 7C 41
Corydalis Cl. LE11: Loug 5G 21
Cosby Dr. LE12: East L 1G 11
COSSINGTON 5F 31
Cossington La. LE7: Coss 6H 31
LE7: R'ley 1C 36
Cossington Rd. LE12: Sileby 3E 31
Costock Rd. LE12: East L 3H 11
COTES 3D 16
Cotes Dr. LE11: Loug 3H 15
Cotes Rd. LE12: Bar S, Cote 4D 16
Cothelstone Av. LE11: Loug 4C 14
Cotswold Cl. LE11: Loug 6D 14
LE13: Mel M 7D 41
Cottage Cl. LE12: East L 1G 11
Cottage Gdns. Cl.
LE12: Hath 6A 10
Cottages, The
LE12: Woodh E 5H 27
Cottesmore Av. LE13: Mel M 4B 40
Cottesmore Cl. LE7: Sys 4C 38
Cottesmore Dr. LE11: Loug 3F 21
Cotton Cft. LE12: Shep 1D 18
Cotton Mill Cres.
LE12: Shep 6E 13
Cotton Way LE11: Loug 2E 15
Countryman's Way
LE7: E Gos 5D 32
Countrymans Way
LE12: Shep 4E 13
County Bri. Mobile Home Pk.
LE12: Hath 4A 10
Courtyard Cl. LE7: Sys 4A 38
Coverdale Cl. LE12: Moun 4A 30
Covert, The LE7: E Gos 5D 32
Covert Cl. LE7: Sys 4G 37
Cowdray Cl. LE11: Loug 2G 21
COW HILL 2F 19
Cowslip Dr. LE12: Shep 6B 12
LE13: Mel M 7A 41
Crabtree Cl. DE74: C Don 3E 5
Cradock Dr. LE12: Quo 6D 22
Cradock St. LE11: Loug 5H 15
Craftsmans Way LE7: E Gos 6D 32
Cramps Cl. LE12: Bar S 4H 23
Craneworks Cl. LE11: Loug 3H 15
Cranmer Dr. LE7: Sys 4H 37
Cranmere Rd. LE13: Mel M 2C 40
Craven Cl. LE11: Loug 4F 21
Craven St. LE13: Mel M 6C 41
Crawshaw Cl. LE12: Long W 4E 9
Crescent, The LE7: R'ley 5A 30
LE12: East L 2H 11
LE13: Mel M 3B 40
Cricketers Dr. LE11: Loug 3G 1
Cricket La. LE11: Loug 3D 2
Croft, The DE74: Keg 3F
Cromwell Dr. LE12: East L 3G 1
Cromwell Rd. LE12: Moun 5H 2
LE13: Mel M 6D 4

Croome Cl. LE11: Loug 2A **22**
CROPSTON 5C **34**
Cropston Av. LE11: Loug 1B **20**
Cropston Rd.
LE7: Anst, Crop 5C **34**
Crossfield Dr. LE13: Mel M 3E **40**
Cross Grn. LE7: R'ley 1A **36**
Cross Hedge LE7: R'ley 6A **30**
Cross Hill La. LE11: Loug 3F **21**
Cross La. LE12: Moun 5H **29**
LE14: Bur L 8F **41**
Crossley Cl. LE12: Bar S 4G **23**
Cross St. LE7: Sys 4B **38**
LE11: Loug 4A **16**
LE12: Hath 6A **10**
Crosswood Cl. LE11: Loug 6C **14**
Crown La. LE12: Moun 2H **29**
Crowson Cl. LE12: Shep 2D **18**
Crowson Dr. LE12: Quo 4E **23**
Cumberland Rd. LE11: Loug . . .5F **15**
Cumberland Trad. Est.
LE11: Loug 5E **15**
Cumbrian Way LE12: Shep 6E **13**
Curlew Cl. LE7: Sys 3H **37**
LE12: Moun 1G **29**
Curzon Cl. LE7: Quen 2D **38**
Curzon St. LE11: Loug 5G **15**
Cygnet Cl. LE7: Sys 3H **37**
LE12: Sileby 2E **31**
Cygnus Ct. DE74: Nott A 5A **6**
Cypress Cl. LE11: Loug 4G **21**
Cypress Rd. LE12: Bar S 2G **23**

D

Dakota Rd. DE74: Nott A 5F **5**
Dalby Av. LE4: Birs 6D **36**
Dalby Rd. LE13: Mel M 5B **41**
LE14: Mel M 8B **41**
Daleacre Av. DE74: Lock 1B **6**
Daleacre Ct. DE74: Lock 1B **6**
Dale Cl. LE4: Birs 6C **36**
Dalley Cl. LE7: Sys 5B **38**
Damson Cl. LE7: R'ley 2B **36**
Damson Dr. LE12: Bar S 2H **23**
Dan Maskell Tennis & Netball Cen.
. . . . .1E **21**
Danvers La. LE12: Shep 5E **13**
Danvers Rd. LE12: Moun 4A **30**
Darcy Gdns. LE13: Mel M 1C **40**
Darsway DE74: C Don 1D **4**
Darwin Cres. LE11: Loug 2B **14**
Dawes Mdw. Rd. LE4: Wan 6B **36**
Deacon Cl. LE12: Shep 6E **13**
Dead La. LE11: Loug 5H **15**
Deanery Cres. LE4: Leic 6H **35**
Deane St. LE11: Loug 4E **15**
Deanside Dr. LE11: Loug 3D **14**
Dean's La. LE12: Woodh E 2A **26**
Dee Cl. LE13: Mel M 4D **40**
Deeming Dr. LE12: Quo 4D **22**
Deepway, The LE12: Quo 6C **22**
Deer Acre LE11: Loug 3H **15**
De Ferrers Cl. LE12: East L 3G **11**
Deighton Way LE11: Loug 3C **14**
De Lacy Ct. DE74: C Don 2E **5**
Delamare Rd. LE13: Mel M 1D **40**
Delisle Ct. LE11: Loug 1B **20**
Delven La. DE74: C Don 2F **5**
De Montfort LE13: Mel M 2C **40**
De Montfort Cl. LE11: Loug 4C **14**
Denegate Av. LE4: Birs 6B **36**
Denton Ri. LE13: Mel M 5E **41**
Derby Rd. DE74: Keg 2E **7**
LE11: Loug 2C **14**
LE12: Hath 4H **9**
Derbyshire Dr. DE74: C Don 1F **5**
Derby Sq. LE11: Loug 5H **15**
Derwent Dr. LE11: Loug 2D **20**
(not continuous)
LE13: Mel M 6B **41**
Derwent Rd. LE12: Bar S 2H **23**
Devonshire La. LE11: Loug 6H **15**
Devonshire Sq. LE11: Loug . . .6H **15**
Dexter Cl. LE12: Quo 4E **23**
Dickens Cl. LE12: Sileby 1F **31**
Dickens Dr. LE13: Mel M 1B **40**
Dieppe Way LE13: Mel M 2B **40**
DISEWORTH 6A **8**
Diseworth Heritage Cen. 6A **8**
Diseworth Rd. DE74: C Don 3E **5**
DISHLEY 3C **14**
Disraeli St. LE12: Quo 5E **23**
Dobney Av. LE7: Quen 1C **38**
Doctor's La. LE13: Mel M 3E **40**
Domont Cl. LE12: Shep 6D **12**
Donington Cvn. Pk.
DE74: C Don 2E **5**
Donington Park Exhibition Cen.
. . . . .5A **4**
Donington Park Motor Racing Circuit
. . . . .4A **4**
DONINGTON PARK SERVICE AREA
. . . . .6B **6**
Donington Grand Prix Collection
. . . . .5B **4**
Dorian Ri. LE13: Mel M 5B **41**
Dormer Ct. LE12: Hath 6A **10**
Dorothy Av. LE13: Mel M 4A **40**
Dorset Dr. LE13: Mel M 8D **41**
Douglas Jane Cl.
LE13: Mel M 3A **40**
Dovecote DE74: C Don 2F **5**
LE12: Shep 5E **13**
Dovecotes, The LE7: Quen 2G **39**
Dovecote St. LE12: Hath 6A **10**
Dovedale Cl. LE13: Mel M 6B **41**
Dover Cl. LE12: Moun 5H **29**
Dove Rd. DE74: Nott A 5G **5**
Dower Ho. Gdns. LE12: Quo . . .5E **23**
Doyle Cl. LE11: Loug 3D **14**
Dragwell DE74: Keg 3F **7**
Drive, The LE12: Woodh E 4F **27**
LE13: Mel M 6C **41**
Drummond Wlk.
LE13: Mel M 2B **40**
(not continuous)
Drypot La. LE12: Long W 5C **8**
Du Cane Cl. LE12: Shep 2C **18**
Dudley Ct. LE12: Sileby 2E **31**
Dudley Whenham Cl.
LE7: Sys 3A **38**
Duke St. LE11: Loug 4H **15**
LE13: Mel M 3E **40**
Dulverton Cl. LE11: Loug 3C **20**
Dulverton Rd. LE13: Mel M 2A **40**
Duncan Way LE11: Loug 3C **14**
Dunholme Av. LE11: Loug 5B **14**
Dunsmore Cl. LE11: Loug 3D **20**
Dunster Rd. LE12: Moun 4H **29**
Durham Cl. LE13: Mel M 7D **41**
Durham Rd. LE11: Loug 3E **15**
Durrell Cl. LE11: Loug 3C **14**
Dwyer Cl. LE7: Sys 5H **37**
Dyers Ct. *LE11: Loug 4A* ***16***
(off Mill La.)

E

Eagles Dr. LE13: Mel M 7B **41**
Easby Cl. LE11: Loug 4B **14**
East Av. LE7: Sys 3C **38**
LE13: Mel M 3A **40**
Eastfield Av. LE13: Mel M 3C **40**
EAST GOSCOTE 6E **33**
E. Goscote Ind. Est.
LE7: E Gos 6C **32**
EAST LEAKE 3H **11**
East Leake Leisure Cen. 2H **11**
East Link Rd. LE11: Loug 1E **21**
East Midlands Aeropark 4E **5**
EAST MIDLANDS AIRPORT 5G **5**
East Orchard LE12: Sileby 4E **31**
E. Side Cft. LE13: Mel M 1D **40**
Eastway DE74: C Don 2F **5**
Eaton Rd. DE74: C Don 2F **5**
Eatough Cl. LE7: Sys 4D **38**
Edelin Rd. LE11: Loug 2H **21**
Eden Cl. LE11: Loug 4C **14**
Edendale Rd. LE13: Mel M 6A **41**
Edinburgh Way LE12: Moun . . .4G **29**
Edmund Rd. LE4: Birs 6B **36**
Edward Phillipps Rd.
LE12: Hath 1B **14**
Edward St. LE11: Loug 4G **15**
Egerton Rd. LE13: Mel M 4D **40**
Egerton Vw. LE13: Mel M 4B **40**
Elderberry Dr. LE7: R'ley 2B **36**
Elgin Dr. LE13: Mel M 3C **40**
Eliot Cl. LE11: Loug 3B **14**
Ellaby Rd. LE11: Loug 3D **14**
Ellis Cl. LE12: Bar S 3A **24**
LE12: Quo 5D **22**
Elm Av. LE12: East L 1G **11**
Elm Cl. LE12: Moun 3A **30**
Elm Gdns. LE12: Moun 4A **30**
Elmhurst Av. LE13: Mel M 2A **40**
Elmhurst Gdns. LE13: Mel M . . .2A **40**
Elms, The LE11: Loug 6A **16**
Elms Dr. LE12: Quo 6D **22**
Elms Gro. LE11: Loug 6A **16**
LE12: Bar S 2H **23**
Elms Rd. LE13: Mel M 4C **40**
Elvin Way LE11: Loug 1D **20**
Empingham Dr. LE7: Sys 4C **38**
Empress Rd. LE11: Loug 5A **16**
Engineers Ct. LE11: Loug 3H **15**
Ennerdale Rd. LE12: Bar S 3H **23**
Epinal Ct. LE11: Loug 4D **14**
Epinal Way LE11: Loug 4D **14**
Epping Dr. LE13: Mel M 2C **40**
Epworth Ct. LE12: Quo 5E **23**
Ervin Way LE7: Quen 1E **39**
Essex Cl. LE13: Mel M 7D **41**
Everest Dr. LE13: Mel M 2A **40**
Ewden Ri. LE13: Mel M 6B **41**
Exeter Cl. LE7: Sys 5C **38**
LE12: East L 3F **11**
Exmoor Cl. LE11: Loug 3D **20**
Exton Cl. LE7: Sys 5C **38**
Eyebrook Cl. LE11: Loug 1B **20**
Eye Kettleby Lakes
LE14: Mel M 8A **41**

F

Factory St. LE11: Loug 6A **16**
LE12: Shep 5D **12**
Fairfield Cl. LE13: Mel M 2D **40**
Fairfield Ct. LE11: Loug 6A **16**
Fair Mead LE12: Moun 5A **30**
Fairmeadows Way
LE11: Loug 4F **21**
Fairmount Dr. LE11: Loug 1E **21**
Fairway Rd. LE12: Shep 6E **13**
Fairway Rd. Sth.
LE12: Shep 2E **19**
Falcon Bus. Pk. LE11: Loug . . .3A **16**
Falcon St. LE11: Loug 4A **16**
Falcon Way LE12: East L 2H **11**
Faldo Dr. LE13: Mel M 1C **40**
Far La. LE12: Norm S 4D **10**
Farley Way LE12: Quo 5C **22**
Farm Dr. LE12: Bar S 3A **24**
Farmers Way LE7: R'ley 2B **36**
Farndale Dr. LE11: Loug 3F **21**
Farnham Cl. LE7: R'ley 6A **30**
Farnham Ct. LE12: Moun 2H **29**
Farnham Rd. LE11: Loug 2H **21**
Farnham St. LE12: Quo 5D **22**
Far Pastures Rd. LE4: Birs 6B **36**
Farrier's Way LE7: E Gos 6D **32**
Farthings, The LE12: Hath 6A **10**
Fearon St. LE11: Loug 5F **15**
Fennel St. LE11: Loug 5H **15**
Fenny Copse La. LE12: Quo 4E **23**
Ferneley Cres. LE13: Mel M . . .2E **40**
Ferneley Ri. LE7: Thru 1F **33**
Fernie Av. LE13: Mel M 4B **40**
Fern Rd. LE12: Hath 6H **9**
Ferrers Cl. DE74: C Don 2E **5**
Ferryman Rd. LE11: Loug 4A **16**
Festival Dr. LE11: Loug 3G **15**
Festival Way LE11: Loug 3G **15**
Field Av. LE12: Shep 3E **13**
Field Cl. LE13: Mel M 6D **41**
Field Crest LE12: Moun 5H **29**
Field Farm Cl. LE11: Loug 2E **21**
Field Ho. LE11: Loug 5E **15**
Fielding Ct. LE11: Loug 5A **16**
Field Leys Way LE4: Wan 6B **36**
Field St. LE12: Shep 5D **12**
Field Vw. LE7: Sys 4G **37**
Fillingate LE7: Wan 4D **36**
Finsbury Av. LE11: Loug 6A **16**
LE12: Sileby 2G **31**
Firs, The LE7: Sys 5A **38**
Firwood Rd. LE13: Mel M 2E **40**
Fisher Cl. LE7: Coss 5F **31**
LE12: East L 2H **11**
Fishpond Way LE11: Loug 5G **21**
Fishpool Way LE12: Bar S 2A **24**
Flanders Cl. LE12: Quo 5D **22**
Flatten Way LE7: Sys 3A **38**
Flaxland LE7: R'ley 6A **30**
Flaxland Cres. LE12: Sileby 3E **31**
Fleming Cl. LE11: Loug 3D **14**
Fleming Dr. LE13: Mel M 2E **40**
Flesh Hovel La. LE12: Quo 2E **23**
Fletcher's Way LE7: E Gos 6D **32**
Flint La. LE12: Bar S 2G **23**
Foden Cl. LE11: Nan 4A **20**
Forest Cl. LE13: Mel M 2C **40**
Forest Ct. LE11: Loug 6G **15**
Forest Dr. LE12: Sileby 1E **31**
Forest Edge LE11: Loug 2E **21**
Foresters Row LE7: E Gos 6D **32**
Forest Rd. LE11: Loug 2E **21**
LE12: Quo 6C **22**
LE12: Woodh, Woodh E . . .3F **27**
Forest Rock Cl.
LE12: Woodh E 4G **27**
Forest St. LE12: Shep 6E **13**
Forge Ct. LE7: Sys 3B **38**
Forge End LE7: R'ley 2A **36**
Forman Rd. LE12: Shep 1D **18**
Forsyth Cl. LE11: Loug 3B **14**
Fort Rd. LE12: Moun 4H **29**
Fosbrook Dr. DE74: C Don 1D **4**
Fosse Way LE7: Rat W, Sys . . .5H **37**
Foundry La. LE7: Sys 4H **37**
Fowke St. LE7: R'ley 1B **36**
Foxcote Dr. LE11: Loug 1A **20**
Fox Covert LE11: Loug 3H **15**
Fox Covert Cl. LE7: Thurc 6G **35**
Foxglove Av. LE13: Mel M 7A **41**
Foxglove Cl. LE7: E Gos 6E **33**
LE12: Moun 3B **30**
Foxhills DE74: Keg 4E **7**
Fox Hollow LE7: Crop 5D **34**
LE7: E Gos 5D **32**
Fox Pk. Mobile Homes
LE12: Bar S 3H **23**
Fox Rd. DE74: C Don 2D **4**
Framland Dr. LE13: Mel M 1C **40**
Francis Dr. LE11: Loug 3C **14**
Frederick Av. DE74: Keg 2E **7**
Frederick Cl. LE7: Quen 1E **39**
Frederick St. LE11: Loug 6G **15**
Freeby Cl. LE13: Mel M 5E **41**
Freehold St. LE11: Loug 5A **16**
LE12: Quo 5F **23**
LE12: Shep 6E **13**
Freeman's Way LE7: E Gos 5E **33**
Freeman Way LE12: Quo 4D **22**
Freesia Cl. LE11: Loug 5G **21**
Freshney Cl. LE13: Mel M 6B **41**
Friar Cl. LE12: Shep 3C **18**
Frith Cl. LE12: East L 1G **11**
Frost Flds. DE74: C Don 1F **5**
Furlong Cl. LE7: Sys 4C **38**
Furrow Cl. LE7: R'ley 1A **36**
LE12: Bar S 2H **23**

G

Gables, The DE74: Dise 5A **8**
Gable's Lea LE12: Sut B 1B **10**
Gaddesby La. LE7: Rear 4G **33**
(not continuous)
Gallico Cl. LE11: Loug 4D **14**
Galsworthy Cres.
LE13: Mel M 1B **40**
Gamble Cl. LE7: Sys 4C **38**
Gamble Way LE12: Quo 4D **22**
Garat's Hay LE12: Woodh 2H **27**
Garden Cres. DE74: C Don 2F **5**
Garden La. LE13: Mel M 2A **40**
Garden Row DE74: Keg 2F **7**
Gardner Cl. LE11: Loug 3C **14**
Gardner Way LE12: Bar S 2F **23**
Garendon Av. LE12: Hath 1A **14**
Garendon Cl. LE12: Shep 6E **13**
Garendon Grn. LE11: Loug 6D **14**
Garendon Park 5A **14**
Garendon Pk. Obelisk 5B **14**
Garendon Rd. LE11: Loug 5D **14**
LE12: Shep 6D **12**
Garland LE7: R'ley 6A **30**
Garthorpe Dr. LE13: Mel M 5E **41**
Garton Rd. LE11: Loug 6H **15**
Gartree Ct. LE13: Mel M 7C **41**
Gartree Dr. LE13: Mel M 6C **41**
Gascoigne Av. LE7: Quen 2E **39**
Gavin Dr. LE11: Loug 3D **14**
Gelders Hall Ind. Est.
LE12: Shep 2C **18**
Gelders Hall Rd.
LE12: Shep 1C **18**
Geoff Monk Way LE4: Wan 5C **36**
George Deacon Ct.
LE11: Loug 5G ***15***
(off Ashby Rd.)
George St. LE11: Loug 5F **15**
LE13: Mel M 4D **40**
George Toon Ct. LE7: Sys 3A **38**

George Yd. LE11: Loug 5H **15**
Georgina Ct. DE74: C Don 1F **5**
Gerrard Cres. DE74: Keg 4F **7**
Gibson Cl. LE12: Shep 5E **13**
Gibson Rd. LE12: Sileby 1F **31**
Gifford Cl. LE4: Birs 6B **36**
Giles Cl. LE12: Quo 1F **29**
Gilpin Cl. LE13: Mel M 6A **41**
Gipsy La. LE7: R'ley 5G **29**
LE12: Bar S 2D **24**
Gisborough Way LE11: Loug . . .4B **14**
Gladstone Av. LE11: Loug 4G **15**
LE13: Mel M 2A **40**
Gladstone St. LE11: Loug 4H **15**
LE12: Hath 6A **10**
Glamis Cl. LE12: Moun 5G **29**
Glebe Cl. LE12: Moun 3H **29**
Glebeland Cl. LE7: Thru 1F **33**
Glebelands Rd. LE4: Leic 6H **35**
Glebe Rd. LE7: Quen 2E **39**
Glebe St. LE11: Loug 4A **16**
Glebe Way LE7: Sys 3G **37**
Glenfields LE12: Shep 6C **12**
Glenfrith Cl. LE12: Moun 4B **30**
Glenfrith Gdns. LE12: Moun 4B **30**
Glenmore Av. LE12: Shep 5C **12**
Glen Rd. LE11: Loug 4H **21**
Gloucester Av. LE7: Sys 3C **38**
LE13: Mel M 7D **41**
Gloucester Cres.
LE13: Mel M 7D **41**
Glover Rd. DE74: C Don 1F **5**
Golden Sq. LE12: Hath 1H **13**
Goldfinch Cl. LE11: Loug 6F **15**
Golding Cl. LE11: Loug 3B **14**
Goldspink Cl. LE13: Mel M 7C **41**
Goode's Av. LE7: Sys 5B **38**
Goode's La. LE7: Sys 4A **38**
Goodriche Ho. *LE13: Mel M . . .4D* ***40***
(off St Johns Ct.)
Goodriche St. LE13: Mel M 4D **40**
Goods Yd. Cl. LE11: Loug 5F **15**
Gordon Rd. LE11: Loug 3A **16**
Gorse Covert Cen.
LE11: Loug 4C **14**
Gorse La. LE7: Sys 4H **37**
Gotham Rd. LE12: East L 1G **11**
Grace Dieu Ct. LE11: Loug 5D **14**
Gracedieu Rd. LE11: Loug 6C **14**
Gracedieu Way LE11: Loug 6D **14**
Grafton Rd. LE11: Loug 3E **15**
Graham Perkins Cl.
LE12: Shep 6D **12**
Graham Ri. LE11: Loug 3D **14**
Granby Ho. *LE13: Mel M 4C* ***40***
(off Greenslade)
Granby Rd. LE13: Mel M 1D **40**
Granby St. LE11: Loug 5G **15**
Grange, The LE12: Woodh E . . .5H **27**
Grange Av. LE7: Rear 5F **33**
Grange Dr. DE74: C Don 2E **5**
LE13: Mel M 5D **41**
Grangefields Dr. LE7: R'ley 1B **36**
Grange La. LE12: Moun 5H **29**
Granger Ct. LE11: Loug 5G **15**
Grange Rd. LE12: Shep 6C **12**
Grange St. LE11: Loug 4G **15**
Granite Way LE7: Sys 5G **37**
LE12: Moun 1G **29**
Grantwood Rd.
LE13: Mel M 2E **40**
Granville Rd. LE13: Mel M 2A **40**
Granville St. LE11: Loug 5G **15**
Grapes Gdn. Cl.
LE12: Moun 2A **30**
Grasmere Cl. LE12: Bar S 3H **23**
Grasmere Rd. LE11: Loug 4F **21**
Grassholme Dr. LE11: Loug . . .1A **20**
Gravel Pit Rd. LE4: Birs 6B **36**
Gray La. LE12: Sileby 3F **31**
Grays Cl. DE74: C Don 2F **5**
Grays Ct. LE12: Bar S 3H **23**
Gray St. LE11: Loug 1H **21**
Great Central Railway
Loughborough Central Station
. . . . .6A **16**
Quorn & Woodhouse Station
. . . . .6B **22**
Rothley Station 2F **35**
Rushcliffe Halt Station . . .1G **11**
Great Central Railway Mus. 6A **16**
Gt. Central Rd. LE11: Loug 6A **16**
Greaves Av. LE13: Mel M 3B **40**
Grebe Cl. LE12: Bar S 3A **24**
Greedon Ri. LE12: Sileby 1E **31**
Green, The DE74: C Don 2D **4**
DE74: Dise 6A **8**
(not continuous)
LE7: Sys 3B **38**
LE7: Thru 1F **33**
LE12: East L 3G **11**
LE12: Hath 6A **10**
LE12: Long W 4E **9**
LE12: Moun 3A **30**
(not continuous)
NG11: King 1H **7**
Green Bank LE13: Mel M 4E **40**
Greenclose La. LE11: Loug 5G **15**
Greenhill LE12: Hath 6A **10**
Greenhill Cl. LE13: Mel M 2D **40**
Greenhill Ri. LE12: Hath 5A **10**
Green La. DE74: Dise 6F **5**, 5A **8**
LE12: Sea 3H **25**
Green La. Cl. LE12: Sea 3H **25**
Greenslade LE13: Mel M 4C **40**
Greensward LE7: E Gos 5E **33**
Greenway Cl. LE7: R'ley 1A **36**
Greetham Way LE7: Sys 4C **38**
Gregory St. LE11: Loug 6H **15**
Gretton Ct. LE13: Mel M 4B **40**
Griffin Cl. LE12: Shep 6C **12**
Griggs Rd. LE11: Loug 3H **21**
Grimes Ga. DE74: Dise . . .6G **5**, 5A **8**
Grove, The LE11: Loug 5E **15**
Grove La. LE12: Bar S 4H **23**
Grove Rd. LE11: Loug 6E **15**
Guadaloupe Av. LE13: Mel M . . .6E **41**
Guild Cl. LE7: Crop 4D **34**
Guildford Way LE11: Loug 3C **20**

H

Haddon Cl. LE7: Sys 4H **37**
Haddon Way LE11: Loug 5G **21**
Hadfield Dr. LE13: Mel M 3C **40**
Hadrian Cl. LE7: Sys 5G **37**
Hailey Av. LE11: Loug 4C **14**
Half Croft, The LE7: Sys 3A **38**
Halford St. LE7: Sys 4A **38**
Halfpenny Cl. LE4: Birs 6C **36**
Halifax Dr. LE13: Mel M 5B **41**
Hall, The LE7: Quen 2G **39**
Hallam Flds. DE74: C Don 3E **5**
Hallam Flds. Rd.
LE4: Birs, Wan 6B **36**
Hallamford Rd. LE12: Shep 2B **12**
Hallam Wlk. LE4: Birs 6B **36**
Hallaton Dr. LE7: Sys 4C **38**
Hall Cl. LE7: Coss 5F **31**
Hall Cft. LE12: Shep 5D **12**
Hall Dr. LE12: Bur W 5G **17**
Hall Farm Cl. DE74: C Don 2E **5**
LE7: Quen 2F **39**
Hall Farm Ct. LE12: Sea 4H **25**
Hall Farm Rd. LE7: Thurc 5F **35**
Hallfields La. LE7: R'ley 1A **36**
Hallfields Wlk. LE7: R'ley 2B **36**
Hall Gdns. DE74: Hem 1H **5**
LE12: East L 4H **11**
Hall Ga. DE74: Dise 6A **8**
Hall Leys LE12: Quo 6E **23**
Halls Brook LE12: East L 2G **11**
Halstead Gdns. LE12: Moun 4H **29**
Halstead Rd. LE12: Moun 4G **29**
Halstead Road Centenary
Pasture Local Nature Reserve
. . . . .4G **29**
Halywell Nook LE7: R'ley 5B **30**
Hambledon Cres.
LE11: Loug 3F **21**
Hames Cl. LE7: R'ley 1C **36**
Hamilton Dr. LE13: Mel M 6C **41**
Hamilton Lawn Tennis Club . . .6C **41**
Hamilton Pl. LE13: Mel M 6C **41**
Hanford Way LE11: Loug 4H **15**
Hanover Ct. LE11: Loug 4D **14**
Hanover Dr. LE12: Sileby 2F **31**
Harcourt Cl. LE7: Sys 3A **38**
Harcourt Pl. DE74: C Don 1F **5**
Hardwick Cres. LE7: Sys 4H **37**
Hardwick Dr. LE11: Loug 5C **14**
Hardy Ct. LE12: Sea 2H **25**
Hardy Way LE12: East L 1G **11**
Harebell Dr. LE13: Mel M 7A **41**
Harefield LE12: East L 1G **11**
Harlech Cl. LE11: Loug 4E **15**
Harlech Wlk. LE13: Mel M 2C **40**
Harlequin Rd. LE12: Sileby 3E **31**
Harley Cl. LE12: Shep 1D **18**
Harriman Cl. LE12: Shep 5D **12**
Harrington Cl. LE12: Quo 5E **23**
Harrington Rd. LE12: Shep 6E **13**
Harrison's Row LE7: Sys 3B **38**
Harrowgate Dr. LE4: Birs 6A **36**
Harry French Ct. LE11: Loug . . .5E **15**
Hartington St. LE11: Loug 5A **16**
Hartland Dr. LE13: Mel M 7C **41**
Hartopp Rd. LE13: Mel M 7C **41**
Harvesters Cnr. LE7: E Gos 6E **33**
Harvey Ct. DE74: C Don 2F **5**
Harvey Rd. DE74: C Don 3F **5**
Harvey St. LE13: Mel M 3D **40**
Hassall M. LE7: Rear 4F **33**
Hastings Rd. LE12: Woodh E . . .5F **27**
Hastings St. DE74: C Don 3F **5**
LE11: Loug 5G **15**
HATHERN 6A **10**
Hathern Dr. LE11: Loug 3H **13**
LE12: Hath 2A **14**
Hathern Rd. LE12: Long W 4F **9**
LE12: Shep 4E **13**
Hathern Turn LE12: Hath 5H **9**
Hathernware Ind. Est.
LE12: Norm S 2C **10**
Haulton Dr. DE74: C Don 1E **5**
Havelock St. LE11: Loug 5F **15**
Haven, The LE11: Loug 4D **14**
Hawcliffe Rd. LE12: Moun 2G **29**
Hawker Cl. LE11: Loug 4D **14**
Hawley Cl. LE12: East L 3H **11**
Hawthorn Av. LE4: Birs 6D **36**
Hawthorn Dr. LE13: Mel M 2C **40**
Hawthorne Av. LE12: Hath 6A **10**
Hawthorn Rd. DE74: C Don 1F **5**
LE12: Moun 3A **30**
Haybrooke Rd. LE12: Sileby 1F **31**
Haydon Rd. LE11: Loug 5E **15**
Hayhill LE12: Bar S 6C **24**
Haymeadow Cl. LE11: Loug . . .3F **21**
Hayward Av. LE11: Loug 1A **22**
Hazel Cl. LE4: Birs 6D **36**
Hazelrigg Cl. DE74: C Don 1D **4**
Hazel Rd. LE11: Loug 3G **21**
Headland, The LE7: E Gos 5F **33**
Heafield Dr. DE74: Keg 3F **7**
Heath Av. LE7: Sys 4H **37**
Heathcoat St. LE11: Loug 5G **15**
Heathcote Dr. LE12: Sileby 1F **31**
Heather Cres. LE13: Mel M 7A **41**
Heavenside LE12: East L 1G **11**
Hedley Cl. LE12: Long W 3C **8**
HEMINGTON 1H **5**
Hemington Ct. DE74: Hem 1G **5**
Hemington Hill DE74: Hem 1G **5**
Hemington La. DE74: Lock 1A **6**
Henry Robson Dr.
LE12: Moun 4A **30**
Herald Way DE74: Nott A 5H **5**
Herbert St. LE11: Loug 4H **15**
Hermitage Rd. LE11: Loug 1B **20**
Heron Cl. LE12: Moun 3B **30**
Heron Rd. LE12: Bar S 3A **24**
Heron's Way LE7: E Gos 5E **33**
Heron Way LE7: Sys 3H **37**
Herrick Cl. LE12: Sileby 2D **30**
Herrick Rd. LE11: Loug 1G **21**
LE12: Woodh E 3F **27**
Herriot Way LE11: Loug 4D **14**
Hertford Cl. LE7: Sys 5C **38**
Hickling Cl. LE7: R'ley 1C **36**
Hickling Ct. LE11: Loug 5F **15**
Hickling Dr. LE12: Sileby 1F **31**
Highbridge LE12: Sileby 2E **31**
Highfield Av. LE13: Mel M 2A **40**
Highfields LE12: Bar S 3H **23**
Highfields Cl. LE12: Shep 4E **13**
Highfields Dr. LE11: Loug 1D **20**
Highfields Rd. LE12: Moun 4H **29**
Highgate Av. LE4: Birs 6A **36**
Highgate Rd. LE12: Sileby 2F **31**
Highland Dr. LE11: Loug 5H **21**
High Mdw. LE12: Hath 6A **10**
Highreeds End LE12: Sileby 6F **25**
High St. DE74: C Don 3E **5**
DE74: Keg 3E **7**
LE7: Sys 3A **38**
LE11: Loug 5H **15**
LE12: Bar S 4H **23**
LE12: Quo 5D **22**
LE12: Sileby 2E **31**
LE13: Mel M 4C **40**
Hilary Cl. LE13: Mel M 1E **40**
Hillcrest Dr. LE11: Loug 4H **21**
Hill Ri. LE12: Woodh E 4F **27**
Hillside DE74: C Don 1F
DE74: Keg 4F **7**
Hillside Av. LE13: Mel M 2A **40**
Hillside Way LE12: Shep 2C **18**
Hill Top DE74: C Don 4D **4**
Hill Top Rd. LE11: Loug 2E **21**
Hobbs Wick LE12: Sileby 2E **31**
Hoby Rd. LE7: Thru 1F **33**
Hockey Cl. LE11: Loug 2G **15**
Hodson Ct. LE11: Loug 1H **21**
Hogarth Rd. LE4: Leic 6G **35**
Holbein Cl. LE11: Loug 5A **16**
Holbourne Cl. LE12: Bar S 4G **23**
Holland Cl. *LE11: Loug 6A* ***16***
(off Trinity St.)
Holland Rd. LE13: Mel M 4A **40**
Hollands Way DE74: Keg 3F **7**
Hollingshead Yd.
LE13: Mel M 4C ***40***
(off Nottingham St.)
Hollis Mdw. LE12: East L 1G **11**
Hollis Way LE12: Hath 6H **9**
Hollow, The DE74: C Don 2F **5**
Hollybush Cl. LE7: Sys 3H **37**
Hollygate Cl. LE13: Mel M 5E **41**
Hollytree Av. LE4: Birs 6C **36**
Hollytree Cl. LE11: Loug 4G **21**
Holmdale Rd. LE7: Sys 4A **38**
Holme Av. LE12: East L 1G **11**
Holmfield Av. LE11: Loug 3F **15**
Holt Dr. LE11: Loug 1F **21**
Holt Ri. LE12: Shep 2E **19**
Holywell Dr. LE11: Loug 2C **20**
Holywell Sports Complex 2C **20**
Holywell Way LE11: Loug 2C **20**
Home Farm Cl.
LE12: Woodh 2A **28**
Home Farm Courtyard
DE74: C Don 2A **4**
Homefield La. LE7: R'ley 1B **36**
Homefield Rd. LE12: Sileby 1E **31**
Homestead, The
LE12: Moun 2A **30**
Homestead Cl. LE7: Coss 5F **31**
Homeway Cl. LE12: Shep 6E **13**
Honeysuckle Cl. LE7: E Gos . . .6F **33**
Honeysuckle Way
LE11: Loug 5G **21**
LE13: Mel M 7A **41**
Hooper Cl. LE11: Loug 4H **21**
Hoppner Cl. LE4: Leic 6H **35**
Hornbeam Cl. LE11: Loug 5G **21**
Hornecroft LE7: R'ley 1A **36**
Horse Fld. Vw. LE13: Mel M . . .2A **40**
Horseguards Way
LE13: Mel M 1A **40**
Horse Shoes, The DE74: Hem . . .1G **5**
Hospital Way LE11: Loug 5E **15**
Houghton Way LE4: Wan 6B **36**
Howard Cl. LE11: Loug 4C **14**
Howard Dr. DE74: Keg 2E **7**
Howard St. LE11: Loug 4H **15**
Howden Cl. LE11: Loug 6B **14**
Howe La. LE7: R'ley 1A **36**
Howe Rd. LE11: Loug 2H **21**
Howgate Cl. LE12: Sileby 5F **25**
Hoyte Dr. DE74: Keg 2E **7**
Hubbard Rd. LE12: Bur W 5H **17**
Hudson Rd. LE12: Sileby 1E **31**
LE13: Mel M 4E **40**
Hudson St. LE11: Loug 5A **16**
Hugh Foss Dr. LE11: Loug 5H **21**
Hugh Lupus Ct.
LE12: Moun 2H **29**
Humber Dr. LE13: Mel M 6B **41**
Humble La. LE7: Coss 5F **31**
Hume St. LE11: Loug 5A **16**
Humphrey Cl. LE11: Loug 1A **22**
Hungarton Dr. LE7: Sys 4C **38**
Hungary La. LE12: Sut B 1B **10**
Hunt Dr. LE13: Mel M 1E **40**
Hunter Rd. DE74: Nott A 5A **6**
Hunters Rd. LE13: Mel M 6D **41**
Huntingdon Cl. LE12: Bur W . . .5G **17**
Huntingdon Ct. LE11: Loug 5G **15**
Huntingdon Dr.
DE74: C Don 1E **5**
Huntsmans Cl. LE12: Quo 4F **23**
Huntsman's Dale
LE7: E Gos 5D **32**
Hunts Orchard LE12: Hath 1A **14**
Hurstwood Rd. LE11: Loug 6B **14**
Huston Cl. LE12: Bar S 5B **24**
Huston Ct. *LE11: Loug 6G* ***15***
(off Wards End)

Regent St.—Station Rd.

Regent St. LE7: Thru 1F 33
LE11: Loug 5G 15
LE13: Mel M 5D 41
Remount Rd. LE13: Mel M 4A 40
Rempstone Rd. LE12: Belt 2A 12
LE12: East L, Stanf S 4F 11
Rendell St. LE11: Loug 4H 15
(not continuous)
Renning End LE12: Moun 5A 30
Reservoir Rd. LE7: Crop 4B 34
Retreat, The LE12: Bar S 3H 23
Revell Cl. LE12: Quo 5F 23
Ribble Dr. LE12: Bar S 5H 23
Ribble Way LE13: Mel M 6B 41
Richard Cl. LE13: Mel M 4D 40
Richmond Dr. LE13: Mel M 7D 41
Ridgemere Cl. LE7: Sys 3D 38
Ridgemere La. LE7: Sys 4E 39
Ridge Way LE12: Bar S 2H 23
Ridgeway, The LE7: R'ley 2F 35
Ridings, The LE7: Quen 2E 39
LE7: R'ley 6E 29
Ridley Cl. LE7: Crop 5D 34
Rigsty, The LE12: Quo 5C 22
Ring Fence LE12: Shep 1D 18
Ringway, The LE7: Quen 1E 39
Ringwood Rd. LE12: Shep 4D 12
Rise, The LE7: R'ley 1C 36
Riverdale Cl. *LE7: Sys 3A 38*
(off Brookside)
Riverside M. LE7: Wan 5E 37
Riverside Rd. LE13: Mel M 4A 40
River Vw. LE12: Bar S 5A 24
Rivington Dr. LE11: Loug 1B 20
Robert Hardy Wharf
LE11: Loug 5B 16
Roberts Cl. DE74: Keg 4F 7
Robin Cres. LE13: Mel M 7B 41
Robin M. LE11: Loug 6G 15
Roby Lea DE74: C Don 1D 4
Rochester Cl. LE12: Moun 5G 29
Rockhill Dr. LE12: Moun 5H 29
Rockingham Cl. LE12: Shep 1C 18
Rockingham Dr.
LE13: Mel M 3A 40
Rockingham Rd. LE11: Loug 3E 15
LE12: Moun 5G 29
Roecliffe Rd. LE7: Crop 3A 34
LE12: Woodh E 3A 34
Roman Cl. LE12: Bar S 2H 23
Romans, The LE12: Moun 4H 29
Roman Way LE7: Sys 5G 37
Romway Cl. LE12: Shep 6E 13
Ronald W. Ct. LE11: Loug 2D 20
Roods, The LE7: R'ley 1A 36
Rookery, The LE12: Bar S 3G 23
Ropewalk LE12: East L 3F 11
Ropewalk, The DE74: Keg 3E 7
Rosebery Av. LE13: Mel M 4D 40
Rosebery St. LE11: Loug 5F 15
Rosebery Way LE11: Loug 5E 15
Rose Dr. LE7: E Gos 5F 33
Rosehill LE11: Loug 5C 14
Roseveare Dr. LE11: Loug 4H 21
Rosewood Way LE11: Loug 5F 21
Rosminian Way LE7: Coss 3H 31
Ross Cl. LE13: Mel M 2E 40
Rossiter Cl. LE13: Mel M 3B 40
Rosslyn Av. LE12: Moun 5G 29
ROTHLEY 1A 36
Rothley Pk. Golf Course 2G 35
ROTHLEY PLAIN 5F 29
Rothley Rd. LE12: Moun 3A 30
Rothley Station
Great Central Railway 2F 35
Rothschild End LE11: Loug 4H 21
Roulstone Cres.
LE12: East L 1G 11
Roundhill Cl. LE7: Sys 5H 37
Roundhill Way LE11: Loug 6B 14
Routh Av. DE74: C Don 3F 5
Rowan Av. LE12: Hath 5A 10
Rowbank Way LE11: Loug 6B 14
Rowe Leyes Furlong
LE7: R'ley 4B 30
Rowena Ct. LE12: Moun 5A 30
Rowlandson Cl. LE4: Leic 6H 35
Royal Way LE11: Loug 3G 15
Roy Brown Dr. LE12: Sileby 2G 31
Roydale Cl. LE11: Loug 3E 15
Royland Rd. LE11: Loug 6H 15
Rubicon Cl. LE12: Moun 4B 30
Rudbeck Av. LE13: Mel M 4A 40
Rudyard Cl. LE11: Loug 1B 20
Rufford Cl. LE11: Loug 4B 14
Rumsey Cl. LE12: Quo 5C 22
Rupert Brooke Rd.
LE11: Loug 5D 14
Rupert Cres. LE7: Quen 1E 39
Rupert Law Cl. LE12: Quo 4D 22
Rushcliffe Gro. LE12: East L 1G 11
Rushcliffe Halt Station
Great Central Railway 1G 11
Rushes, The LE11: Loug 5G 15
Rushes Shop. Cen., The
LE11: Loug 5G 15
Rushey La. LE7: R'ley 3F 29
LE12: Woodh 3A 28
Ruskin Av. LE7: Sys 5C 38
Russ Cl. LE12: Quo 4D 22
Russell St. LE11: Loug 5A 16
Russett Way LE4: Birs 6E 37
Russet Way LE13: Mel M 2B 40
Rutland Ho. *LE13: Mel M 4D 40*
(off Rutland St.)
Rutland St. LE11: Loug 6A 16
LE13: Mel M 4D 40
Rydal Av. LE11: Loug 2D 20
Ryegate Cres. LE4: Birs 6B 36
Ryeholme Cl. LE12: East L 1H 11

S

Saddle Cl. LE13: Mel M 2A 40
Saddlers Cl. LE11: Loug 3F 15
Saddlers' Cl. LE7: E Gos 6D 32
Saddlers Ct. LE13: Mel M 4D 40
Sage Cross St. LE13: Mel M 4C 40
St Aidan's Av. LE7: Sys 4H 37
St Andrews Cl. LE12: Bur W 5H 17
St Andrew's Ri. DE74: Keg 4E 7
St Annes Cl. LE7: Sys 5C 38
St Anne's La. DE74: C Don 2F 5
LE12: Sut B 1B 10
St Anthonys Wlk. LE7: Sys 5C 38
St Bartholomews Way
LE14: Mel M 1A 40
St Benets Wlk. *LE7: Sys 5D 38*
(off Linacre Cres.)
St Bernard's Cl. LE12: Shep 6C 12
St Botolph Rd. LE12: Shep 6D 12
St Columba Way LE7: Sys 3H 37
St Cross Wlk. *LE7: Sys 5D 38*
(off Somerville Cl.)
St Edmunds Wlk. LE7: Sys 5D 38
St Edward's Rd. DE74: C Don 3F 5
St Gregorys Dr. LE12: Sileby 2F 31
St Hilda's Cl. LE7: Sys 5C 38
St Hughs Wlk. *LE7: Sys 5D 38*
(off Somerville Cl.)
St James Cl. LE12: Shep 1D 18
St James Rd. LE12: Shep 6D 12
St John's Av. LE7: Sys 4C 38
St Johns Ct. LE13: Mel M 4D 40
St Johns Dr. LE13: Mel M 2C 40
St Leonards Cl.
LE12: Bur W 5H 17
LE13: Mel M 4A 40
St Mary's Cl. LE11: Loug 5F 15
LE13: Mel M 4C 40
(off St Mary's Way)
St Marys Cl. LE12: Bur W 5H 17
St Mary's Cres. LE12: East L 1G 11
St Mary's Rd. LE12: Sileby 1E 31
St Mary's Way LE13: Mel M 4C 40
St Olaves Cl. LE11: Loug 4B 14
St Pauls Ct. LE7: Sys 3B 38
St Paul's Dr. LE7: Sys 5A 38
St Peter's Av. LE12: Hath 6A 10
St Peter's Ct. LE7: Sys 3B 38
St Peter's St. LE7: Sys 4A 38
St Peters Wlk. LE13: Mel M 3B 40
St Philips Rd. LE12: Bur W 5H 17
St Winefride Rd.
LE12: Shep 6D 12
St Winifreds Ct. NG11: King 1H 7
Saley Cl. LE12: Shep 2D 18
Salisbury Av. LE12: East L 3H 11
LE13: Mel M 3D 40
Salisbury St. LE11: Loug 5A 16
Salmon M. LE12: Shep 5D 12
Salter Cl. DE74: C Don 1D 4
Saltersgate Dr. LE4: Birs 6C 36
Sandalwood Rd. LE11: Loug 2E 21
Sanders Rd. LE12: Quo 5D 22
Sandford Rd. LE7: Sys 4A 38
Sandgate Av. LE4: Birs 6B 36
Sandham Bri. Rd. LE7: Crop 4D 34
Sandhills, The LE12: Quo 5C 22
Sandhole La. LE12: Shep 2A 18
Sandpit Dr. LE4: Wan 6B 36
Sandringham Dr.
LE11: Loug 4D 14
Sandringham Ri.
LE12: Shep 1B 18
Sandy La. LE13: Mel M 6C 41
LE14: Mel M 6C 41
Sapcote Ct. LE13: Mel M 6D 41
Sapcote Dr. LE13: Mel M 6E 41
Sarson St. LE12: Quo 5D 22
Saville Dr. LE12: Sileby 3E 31
Saxby Dr. LE7: Sys 5C 38
Saxby Rd. LE13: Mel M 4D 40
LE14: Bren 4D 40
Saxby Rd. Ind. Est.
LE13: Mel M 4E 40
Saxon Dr. LE7: R'ley 2B 36
Saxon Way LE12: Bar S 2H 23
Scalford Rd. LE13: Mel M 1C 40
Schofield Rd. LE11: Loug 6C 14
School Grn. LE12: East L 3G 11
School La. DE74: C Don 1E 5
LE7: Quen 2F 39
LE12: Quo 6E 23
LE12: Woodh 3H 27
School St. LE7: R'ley 1B 36
LE7: Sys 3B 38
LE11: Loug 5H 15
SEAGRAVE 3H 25
Seagrave Rd. LE7: Thru 1F 33
LE12: Sileby 1E 31
Seals Cl. LE12: Bur W 5H 17
Sedgefield Dr. LE7: Sys 4G 37
Selbourne Ct. LE11: Loug 5A 16
Selbourne St. LE11: Loug 5A 16
Selina Cl. DE74: C Don 1E 5
Selvester Dr. LE12: Quo 6F 23
Senator Cl. LE7: Sys 5H 37
Seton Cl. LE11: Loug 3C 14
Severn Hill LE13: Mel M 6B 41
Seward St. LE11: Loug 6G 15
Seymour Cl. LE11: Loug 4B 14
Seymour Rd. LE12: Bur W 5G 17
Shakespear Cl. DE74: Dise 6A 8
Shakespeare Dr. DE74: Dise 5A 8
Shakespeare St. LE11: Loug 5H 15
Sharpley Dr. LE12: East L 1H 11
Sharpley Rd. LE11: Loug 1B 20
Sharter Dr. LE11: Loug 3B 14
Shearers Ct. *LE11: Loug 4A 16*
(off Mill La.)
Sheepcote LE7: R'ley 6A 30
Sheep Plank La.
LE12: East L 2H 11
Sheldon Cl. LE11: Loug 3B 14
Shelley Av. LE13: Mel M 1B 40
Shelley St. LE11: Loug 4D 14
SHELTHORPE 2H 21
Shelthorpe Av. LE11: Loug 2H 21
Shelthorpe Golf Course 4H 21
Shelthorpe Ho. LE11: Loug 3H 21
Shelthorpe Rd. LE11: Loug 2H 21
Shepherd's Cl. LE12: Sut B 2C 10
Shepherds Cl. LE11: Loug 2D 20
LE12: Shep 4E 13
Shepherds Cft. LE13: Mel M 2B 40
Shepherd's Wlk. LE7: E Gos 6D 32
Shepherd Wlk. DE74: Keg 4E 7
SHEPSHED 5D 12
Shepshed Rd. LE12: Hath 1G 13
Sherrard Dr. LE12: Sileby 4E 31
Sherrard St. LE13: Mel M 4C 40
Sherwood Ct. LE12: Long W 3C 8
Sherwood Dr. LE13: Mel M 3A 40
Shields Cres. DE74: C Don 2D 4
Shirley Cl. DE74: C Don 1E 5
Shirley Dr. LE7: Sys 2B 38
Shirreffs Cl. LE12: Bar S 3A 24
Shooting Cl. La.
LE12: Bar S 4H 23
Short La. DE74: C Don 1C 4
Sibson Dr. DE74: Keg 3D 6
Side Ley DE74: Keg 2E 7
Sidings Wlk. LE11: Loug 4A 16
SILEBY 2E 31
Sileby Rd. LE12: Bar S 4H 23
LE12: Moun, Sileby 2A 30
Sileby Rd. Ind. Est.
LE12: Bar S 5B 24
Sileby Station (Rail) 2E 31
Silver Birches LE12: Quo 5D 22
Silver Birch Way LE7: E Gos 5E 33
Silverbirch Way LE11: Loug 5G 21
Silverton Rd. LE11: Loug 3F 21
Simons Dr. LE12: Sileby 2E 3
Simpson Cl. LE7: Sys 5G 3
Sir Robert Martin Ct.
LE11: Loug 4D 1
Skevington Av. LE11: Loug 5E 1
Skylark Av. LE12: Moun 4B 3
Slash La.
LE12: Bar S, Sileby 6B 2
Smithy La. LE12: Long W 5C
Smithy Way LE12: Shep 5E 1
Snell's Nook La. LE11: Nan 2A 2
Snowdon Cl. LE12: Shep 1E 1
Snow Hill LE13: Mel M 4C 4
Soarbank Way LE11: Loug 2E 1
Soar Cl. LE13: Mel M 6B 41
Soar La. LE12: Norm S 4D 1
LE12: Sut B 5G 7
Soar Rd. LE12: Quo 5F 2
Soar Valley Leisure Cen. 3A 3
Soho St. LE13: Mel M 4C 40
Solway Cl. LE13: Mel M 6B 41
Somerset Cl. LE12: Bur W 5G 17
LE13: Mel M 8D 41
Somerville Cl. LE7: Sys 5D 38
Sorrel Ct. LE12: Moun 3A 30
South Charnwood Leisure Cen.
2C 38
Sth. Croxton Rd. LE7: Quen 2G 39
Southdown Rd. LE11: Loug 4G 2
SOUTH END 3B 3
Southfield Av. LE7: Sys 4B 38
LE12: Sileby 6F 2
Southfield Rd. LE11: Loug 6H 15
South Pde. *LE13: Mel M 4C 4*
(off King St.
South St. LE11: Loug 6H 1
LE12: Bar S 4H 2
Southwell Cl. LE12: East L 3G 1
LE13: Mel M 1A 4
Sovereign Ct. LE11: Loug 6H 1
Sowters La. LE12: Bur W 5H 1
Sparrow Hill LE11: Loug 5H 1
Speeds Pingle LE11: Loug 5G 1
Speedwell Rd. LE12: Moun 3B 3
Spindle Rd. LE11: Loug 5G 2
Spinners Way LE12: Shep 6D 1
Spinney, The DE74: C Don 1E
Spinney Cl. LE7: Sys 4G 3
LE13: Mel M 2E 4
Spinney Dr. LE12: Quo 6D 2
Spinney Hill Dr. LE11: Loug 1D 2
Spital Hill DE74: C Don 1E
Spitfire Rd. DE74: C Don 2D
Spittal, The DE74: C Don 1E
Spring Cl. LE12: Shep 1E 1
Springfield DE74: Keg 3D
Springfield Cl. LE7: R'ley 6A 3
LE11: Loug 3E 2
LE12: Bur W 5G 1
Springfield Rd. LE12: Shep 6C 1
LE12: Sileby 1F 3
Springfield St. LE13: Mel M 2B 4
Spring La. LE12: Long W 5F
LE12: Shep 1D 1
Spruce Av. LE11: Loug 4F 2
Spruce Sq. LE12: Bar S 2G 2
Square, The LE12: Long W 3D
Squire's Ride LE7: E Gos 5D 3
Squirrel's Cnr. LE7: E Gos 5E 3
Squirrel Way LE11: Loug 1F 2
Stableford Cl. LE12: Shep 5D 1
Stafford Av. LE13: Mel M 3D 4
Staffords Acre DE74: Keg 3E
Stamford Dr. LE7: Crop 5D 3
Stanage Rd. LE12: Sileby 1G 3
Stanford Hill LE11: Loug 3H 1
Stanford La. LE12: Cote 1B 1
STANFORD ON SOAR 6H 1
Stanford Rd. LE12: Norm S 5E 1
Stanley St. LE11: Loug 1H 2
LE13: Mel M 4D 4
Starch Cl. LE12: East L 3G 1
Starkie Av. DE74: C Don 2D
Station Av. LE11: Loug 4F 1
Station Blvd. LE11: Loug 3H 1
Station Rd. DE74: C Don 1F
DE74: Keg 2F
DE74: Sut B 2G
LE7: Crop, R'ley 5C 3
LE7: Rear 2G 3
(not continuous
LE12: East L 3F 1
LE12: Quo 5E 2
LE12: Sut B 2G
NG11: King 1H

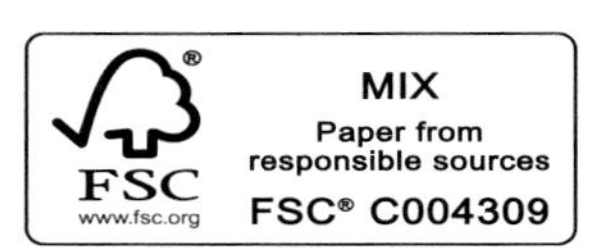

SAFETY CAMERA INFORMATION

PocketGPSWorld.com's CamerAlert is a self-contained speed and red light camera warning system for SatNavs and Android or Apple iOS smartphones/tablets. Visit www.cameralert.com to download.

Safety camera locations are publicised by the Safer Roads Partnership which operates them in order to encourage drivers to comply with speed limits at these sites. It is the driver's absolute responsibility to be aware of and to adhere to speed limits at all times.

By showing this safety camera information it is the intention of Geographers' A-Z Map Company Ltd. to encourage safe driving and greater awareness of speed limits and vehicle speed. Data accurate at time of printing.